Advancing Conversations: Srećko Horvat

Subversion!

Advancing Conversations: Srećko Horvat

Subversion!

Alfie Bown

Winchester, UK
Washington, USA

First published by Zero Books, 2017
Zero Books is an imprint of John Hunt Publishing Ltd., Laurel House, Station Approach,
Alresford, Hants, SO24 9JH, UK
office1@jhpbooks.net
www.johnhuntpublishing.com
www.zero-books.net

For distributor details and how to order please visit the 'Ordering' section on our website.

Text copyright: Alfie Bown 2016

ISBN: 978 1 78535 496 0
978 1 78535 497 7 (ebook)
Library of Congress Control Number: 2016949325

A CIP catalogue record for this book is available from the British Library.

Design: Stuart Davies

Printed and bound by CPI Group (UK) Ltd, Croydon, CR0 4YY, UK

We operate a distinctive and ethical publishing philosophy in all
areas of our business, from our global network of authors to
production and worldwide distribution.

CONTENTS

Introduction

This book is about the politics of subversion and how to do something to help enact change in an ostensibly unarable political landscape. It is also about a global crisis which is not so much on its way as already here, already lived through – to very varying degrees – by all of us. The book, which attempts to develop a global approach to our political problems today, comes out of a Europe whose streets are increasingly lined with army and police presence, whose treatment of its enemies and imagined enemies is increasingly hardline and whose political choices are increasingly responsible for homelessness, war and destruction, not only of beliefs and ideas but of lives and communities. The book therefore sets out with a huge task to complete, and can only hope to be the beginning of more conversations that could assist us in the disastrous situation we find ourselves in today.

Writing its introduction represents a particular kind of personal challenge for me. I came to the work of Srećko Horvat via his books and his articles for publications such as *The Guardian, Al Jazeera, Eutopia* and *OpenDemocracy* among other left-wing and mainstream-left publications. In a world of increasingly prevalent "radical" opinions both on the Left and the Right, most of what I encounter on my newsfeeds and Internet searches (themselves governed and organized by political and corporate hegemonies) strikes me as far less innovative and nuanced than each of us believe ourselves to be. Polemical articles put out by the Left are often underpinned by the same humanism and values that they appear to oppose, often rendering them innocuous at best and at worst, feeding the very structures that they attempt to oppose. Other more highly philosophical approaches might be more "theoretically sound" but lack the praxis to apply on the ground and have real positive effects.

1

Against this backdrop I read the articles and arguments put forward by Srećko Horvat, and found, for once, that almost every idea presented was not only new but potentially useful. All I can really say by way of introduction was that it was my task to bring together some of these ideas, extend them, and spread them to as wide an audience as I could. I hope that the reader will find among these pages, as I did in all of Srećko's work, ideas that they can use, implement and build upon themselves.

Since at least 2012, Srećko has been responding to what he has called "Europe's current deadlock."[1] This deadlock, despite the appearance of a more radical and open political spectrum in Europe, is still very much with us. The challenge he sets forward, for himself and for the rest of us, is to overcome a variety of impasses that we face as members of the Left today. To do this we need politics, we need direct action, and we need philosophy. Using a useful and necessary blend of philosophy and praxis, which, he shows, ought never to be separated, he sets out a number of ways in which we might be able to change things. This book brings together these ideas across three interviews that were recorded over a great many hours of conversation and discussion. Ostensibly, these interviews fell into three categories – politics, love and technology – but as the book shows, these categories are preliminary and ultimately to be dissolved.

At the time of going to print, Srećko is 33 years old and has already been politically active, and even prominent, for nearly a decade. His career is nothing short of remarkable, and he has published over a dozen books in Croatian, French, German and English. By 2007 he was considered a prominent figure in the post-Yugoslavian Left and has always worked internationally to collaborate between nations. He has continued work related to the Balkan states and in 2013 he hosted a TV show that attempted to create a new pan-Balkan identity by overcoming nationalist divides, something he has written about many times since.[2] The attempt ended in controversy and the Bosnian writer Miljenko

Jergović wrote of the show's cancellation:

> The TV show wouldn't be removed if there hadn't been for the Guardian piece. If he had written it in 1942 he would end up in Jasenovac concentration camp. If he had written it in 1972 he would end up in Lepoglava prison. But in 2014 he only lost his TV show because he wrote the truth about Croatia.[3]

This shows several things. First, that Srećko has always written and said what others refrain from saying. Second, it demonstrates his internationalism, another consistent throughout his career. In 2008 he had risen to further prominence and become a central organizer of the Subversive Festival, which is not without controversies of its own, explored in the interviews below. His work to unite nations in new ways has continued and is at its peak today, when Srećko is working closely with Julian Assange's WikiLeaks and with Yanis Varoufakis as a central member of the DiEM25 movement, the most significant European attempt to enact a political move towards real and direct democracy across Europe in place of the false democracies that govern politics at the moment. DiEM25 consistently offers fresh approaches to rising nationalisms, technological control and corporate governance, all of which are explored in this text. Penning this in the days after the UK Brexit vote in which 52% of UK citizens opted to leave the European Union, its work seems more important than ever. The EU is not doing its job, but only the Right have risen to provide viable alternatives that the people are choosing, and Srećko's work urges us to create left-wing responses to the situation.

Another important and unique element of Srećko's work, to my mind, is his work in providing and building platforms for collaboration with a wide range of people. Whilst a philosopher of his credence and reputation could sit back and wait for occasional invitations to share his theoretical insights, Srećko does the opposite. He consistently works to create new platforms, bringing new people into conversation with one another and endlessly working to spread and disseminate useful discussions as far and wide as possible. Every time I spoke to Srećko in the six months it took us to put this manuscript together, he was organizing a new event, project or collaboration. As well as the Subversive Festival and the World Social Forum, he has hosted and shared debates and conversations with almost all of the prominent intellectual figures across the world, from Slavoj Žižek and Noam Chomsky to Francis Fukuyama, Oliver Stone and Julian Assange. Only in June 2016 he was the main coordinator of the "First They Came for Assange" event which took place simultaneously in 14 cities, a central figure in putting together the Show and a key part of a new *Al Jazeera* documentary on the European Crisis. This work, for me, is as invaluable as any personal philosophical writing and, in a climate which increasingly seeks to divide us, can potentially bring us back together to organize change.

The title of Srećko's event "First They Came for Assange" comes from a poem from the 1940s by German pastor Martin Niemöller, which Srećko read out at the event. The poem, written from a concentration camp by a man who had previous supported the Nazis, reads like this:

First they came for the Socialists, and I did not speak out—
    Because I was not a Socialist.
Then they came for the Trade Unionists, and I did not speak
    out—
    Because I was not a Trade Unionist.
Then they came for the Jews, and I did not speak out—
    Because I was not a Jew.
Then they came for me—and there was no one left to speak
    out for me.

Explaining the choice of title, Srećko paraphrased the poem and re-framed it as a historical lesson for today:

> First they came for Julian Assange, and we did not speak out—
> Then they came for Chelsea Manning, and we did not speak out—
> Then they came for Edward Snowden, and we did not speak out—
> Then they came for us—and there was no one left to speak out for us.

This shows that whilst Srećko's work is about philosophy, politics and theory, it is also – and more simply – about helping people out of political crisis. His recent project is not only about Assange or Snowden, but about speaking out for all and everyone and for justice and truth everywhere. Srećko's aim in his writing and in his creation of platforms for others is to help us speak out against everything that oppresses and controls us, before it really is too late.

These are my only introductory comments which explain how I came to Srećko's work and why I chose to approach him to propose this project. I get the impression that he never turns down an opportunity to do something that could be politically useful and I can only hope that our book can do justice to this ambition. Working on it has been one of the most difficult things I have done and has involved changing my mind about a great many things and thinking again about much of what I thought I knew. In many ways it has been a greater challenge than writing any of my own books, and indeed I hope it can be more useful. What follows are the three interviews and my final reflections on the project.

– Alfie Bown, Hong Kong, June 2016

Interview One: Politics

Alfie Bown: In your book co-written with Slavoj Žižek, *What Does Europe Want?* (Columbia University Press, 2014), you describe a global situation today in which there is no unity left, only decay that inevitably leads to disaster.[4] Can I open with a general question and one that is a bit trendy at the moment: is it inevitable that capitalism is leading to disaster? Is this a crisis or disaster *for* capitalism, or the disaster *that is* capitalism, or both? How does this relate to your idea of "permanent civil war"? How bleak is our political situation today?

Srećko Horvat: Although *What Does Europe Want?* was published in 2014, it seems that only a year later all its darkest fears and warnings were, unfortunately, coming true. All that Slavoj and I did, is that we had been closely reading symptoms of Europe's disintegration and concluded that, if there isn't a radical change, Europe would soon diminish. And then came 2015, a year which was even more characterized by what Antonio Gramsci, in his *Prison Notebooks*, called "morbid symptoms."[5] There he says that the old world is dying and that the new world cannot be born yet, and it is at this moment that a series of "morbid symptoms" appear. We live precisely in such an "Interregnum" today. One of the morbid symptoms was the case of Greece which started with huge enthusiasm because of Syriza's victory in January 2015 and ended up, after the historical OXI referendum in July 2015, in a new defeat of the Left which accepted and now implements even worse austerity measures then previous Greek governments. So this was just one of the morbid symptoms of capitalism, where even a democratically elected government had to go against its own political principles and against the will of its own people. Another of the symptoms of disintegration is the still ongoing war in Syria. Another is the refugee crisis which won't end so soon, with more than five million displaced Syrians of which more than one million entered the EU only in the last months of 2015. Not to mention all the refugees from Iraq, Afghanistan, Sudan, Somalia and other war-torn countries which are rarely mentioned anymore. And then, of course, another symptom of this permanent crisis is terrorism, from Paris to Brussels, cities which after the attacks in 2015 look like war zones, with armies on the streets and frequent "terrorist alarms" during the week. At the same time you have the rise of the far-right parties and even governments – Hungary, Poland, Croatia, just to name a few – across Europe. And then in 2016 came Brexit as a final nail in the coffin of Europe as we knew it. We can see new borders, walls, fences, terrorism, displacement of whole populations. So, yes, all these symptoms point in the direction that we really live in a permanent state of civil war or, we could even go so far as to say, permanent war. It is the Italian philosopher Giorgio Agamben who recently proposed the theory of *stasis*.[6] He says that we live in a new phase where civil war is a paradigm for our current situation. And I think today's Europe – but also other parts of the world – perfectly fits into this definition.

AB: So you are saying, via Agamben, that the concept of civil war need no longer refer to a concrete example of a nation fighting within itself but to the condition of Europe as a whole? Is it rather that civil war describes the structural condition of Europe today?

SH: Yes, I am afraid that's correct. So, Agamben calls this *stasis*, which is actually a term from Ancient Greece. In the 4th and 5th century BC, there was a struggle inside the Ancient Greek society between the oligarchic and democratic factions, so it was the city's struggle against internal revolt. What I think we have today is a general experience of this situation on a global level. In what sense? Well, in the sense, firstly, that we have a lot of wars going on in the world at the moment. If you take the case of the war in Syria: it has more than 20 different players involved. These range from the US to Russia, from China to the EU, from Saudi Arabia to Qatar to Israel and so on. All of these players are involved on a geo-political level in the bloody game in Syria. So you can expect that this war also has at least some affects in all of these countries, and you can expect consequences in all these regions, because we live in a globalized and hyper-connected world.

How did the war in Syria start in the first place? It started already with Libya. How did that war start? It started, as was revealed by Hilary Clinton's emails recently made public by WikiLeaks, because the US and France had interest in natural resources and because Western oil companies were heavily indebted to Gaddafi. At one point Gaddafi even proposed to them – what the Troika never proposed to Greece – that they could re-negotiate the debt and even offered to get rid of the debt, but they did not want to do that, so the civil war started. So after the civil war in Libya, part of the arms and so-called "freedom fighters" went to Mali where again France had an interest in natural resources, some went to Niger where wars started as well, and some went to Syria. And why Syria? For at least two reasons. The first is that in Syria, before the so-called "Arab Spring," new natural resources were found, and the second is that Syria was the only country in the Middle East that was not indebted to any international monetary institution. That was a big problem, because you need indebted countries to keep the system running. Then there are Russian interests, Turkish interests, US interests, Israeli interests, etc. This is close to Agamben's definition of *stasis* but it is still not *stasis:* you could still say that these are just "normal" geo-political conditions and that they have occurred many times throughout history, where there have always been wars between countries for land and resources. But when you come to the refugee crisis or terrorism, as two consequences of these wars, then these conditions develop into *stasis*. Why? Because the war, as a boomerang, returns home – precisely where it started.

If you have this situation that we just described, and then on top of that millions of people are forced to flee, and on the other hand, terrorism starts to occur all around Europe, then as a result you have a massive increase in militarization. Just a few days after the attacks in France, in the UK there was a 15% increase in military spending, while there were 20% cuts in other budgets. Then David Cameron decided to abolish the divide between the army and the police and sent ten thousand troops onto the streets of Britain. At the same time, if you walk the streets of Paris or Brussels today you can see not police but the army on every corner. This is quickly becoming a new "normal" and it reminds me of Alfonso Cuaron's wonderful dystopian movie *Children of Men* (2006) in which terrorism, the army and refugees are in full view all the time but no one is surprised any more. It was supposed to be science-fiction, but obviously we are living in a documentary version of *Children of Men* today. All these "morbid symptoms" point in the direction that we are really heading towards what Agamben calls *stasis*. It is this combination of symptoms that defines our condition today. It is no longer a war between individual states but an eruption of the contradictions of capitalism itself. On the one hand you have capitalism's interests because of which France and other countries intervene in other countries for oil and other reasons. On the other hand, you have reactions either in the form of the retreat to the nation-state (rising right-wing extremism, closing of borders, Brexit, etc.) or Islamic fundamentalism. The situation is rapidly accelerating and leading towards war.

Actually – don't be surprised – here I completely agree with Pope Francis, who after the Paris attacks said that we are already living in a Third World War. What I want to add to that comment by Pope Francis is this: what if the Third World War is different and still invisible, although it is highly visible on every corner, because it is not a war that was declared? You can see the symptoms of it, just take a closer look, but no one calls it a Third World War: the refugee crisis, wars, austerity measures, rise of fascism all over Europe, what are all these but symptoms of a permanent war? The symptoms are everywhere, but the war is not declared and probably it is not going to be declared, which makes it particularly difficult to create a kind of resistance movement.

AB: I want to go back to a lot of things you mention here, especially the refugee crisis and the rise of Nazism again today. But first let me ask you about *Children of Men*. Do you know Mark Fisher's discussion of the film?[7] Here it is used as an example of how we cannot think of alternatives to capitalism but only apocalypse. This takes us back to that earlier question of inevitability. Can we think about alternatives and articulate them, or are we stuck in a situation in which every alternative we imagine is yet another dream of capitalism or something like that? What is the position of the Left in this situation?

SH: If there is one lesson we need to learn from Greece it is the old lesson that we always seem to forget: that there can be no communism within one country, or – to paraphrase it – there can be no democracy in only one country. I really despise the fact that much of the Left exclusively blamed Prime Minister Alexis Tsipras for being a traitor and betraying Syriza. Of course, Tsipras was responsible and he could have had many different decisions, but I think we should also speak about our responsibility. There was a kind of international "masturbation" when Syriza came to power, and then a day later when it had all gone wrong no one was blaming themselves, we all only blamed Tsipras. This is a big problem with the Left and it always has been. The Left usually projects its own fantasies and its own hopes onto different political subjects, be that a leader, a movement, a party or something else (for example Tsipras, Occupy Wall Street, the Arab Spring). Then when it doesn't happen, the Left goes down into what Walter Benjamin calls "Left-Wing Melancholy."[8] This is like a sort of incapability to act at all. To come back to the beginning of what I was saying: there are several lessons here. The first and most important one, as I mentioned, is that it is not possible to radically change the situation in one country just by taking power in that country. It is surprising that the Left has not realized this yet. We live in a globalized world and Greece is part of a bigger geo-political situation, so no national government alone can defeat capitalism.

There is a beautiful scene in Costa-Gavras's movie *Capital* (2012) in which a CEO of a big French bank has a family lunch. During the lunch his uncle who is an old '68 guy says: "Nephew, do you know what you are doing in Greece, it brings thousands of people to their knees, creates huge unemployment, high suicide rates and disaster." So the nephew – the banker – responds: "You know uncle, we are actually realizing the dreams you had in 1968." The uncle is astonished and completely surprised, and asks what on earth the nephew means. The nephew says: "We are building internationalism and it's the internationalism of Capital." This shows us the problem of the Left: yes, we need to take power in each country in Europe and beyond, but this is not near enough. If Syriza was in power and at the same time Podemos was in power and Corbyn's Labour was in power in the UK, would the situation have been better? Yes, in a way, they would have had a bit more support in Europe. Do you remember how from the very start of the Syriza government, Alexis Tsipras and Yanis Varoufakis built relationships with Hollande and Renzi, expecting that those two would support them. In the end the Eurogroup was just playing the good-cop/bad-cop routine and they all betrayed Syriza in the end. Perhaps if Jeremy Corbyn and Pablo Iglesias were the allies of Syriza from the beginning, the power balance in the Eurogroup meetings would have been different, but I think this would also not be enough. Two or three countries in Europe with a left government will not really be enough. On the one hand, Syriza had to deal with the domestic oligarchy, with what Andre Gunder Frank calls the *lumpenbourgoisie*. On the other hand, you have to defeat the international monetary system. If you have these two enemies at home and on the international level at the same time, not to mention the rise of right-wing groups, you need more strength.

AB: Did Syriza have real leverage? Were they serious about autarky and was that really going to happen? Or was the whole thing just a case of the good-cop/bad-cop routine that you just mentioned – which was never going to be successful?

SH: I knew Alexis Tsipras and Yanis Varoufakis, and many other members from Syriza, even before they came to power in Greece. Already in 2013 we all met at the Subversive Festival in Zagreb. These people had honest intentions and Syriza back in that year presented a big hope for all of us around Europe. Perhaps in some way we were naive to believe they could achieve the change they announced, and perhaps they were naïve to think that they could defeat the irrationality of capitalism by putting rational arguments on the table in front of those in the Eurozone. But I think what most of the people don't realize – under the false illusion given by the media that Greeks were "lazy" and that Syriza was a completely incapable party – is that in the first months of the Syriza government you had some of the most radical changes that were implemented anywhere throughout Europe in such a short period. Let me give some examples. I had the chance to speak to the Minister of Welfare during my days in Athens in summer 2015. Greece was and still is a country that is in a financial and a humanitarian crisis, so the Ministry of

Welfare is a very important one. First, they started the scheme of food vouchers, so that each month people could go to the supermarket with a card like a credit card and the government would help people to survive by providing food. So what Syriza, in the early days, only several weeks after coming to power, did was a re-invention of the social state or welfare state. Second, they reconnected the electricity for hundreds of thousands of people who had been cut off for failing to pay bills, by making a deal with electricity companies. Third, they passed a law to grant citizenship to all the children of immigrants. All of these acts are more radical than the highly publicized event of Angela Merkel inviting one million people to Germany at the end of 2015. The real question here is: what happened to all these progressive laws? The answer is that when the Memorandum was signed, one of the key points was that all of the laws passed by Syriza would be suspended. So from all these examples, which show a genuine attempt to do something, we can learn that it is not enough to gain power in one country because actually you do not have real power in that country. So what I am claiming – and I think this could be a way out of the problem – is that we need to develop a new internationalism.

AB: So this new internationalism could be a way out of the situation – a way to get real leverage for change, as opposed to these localized attempts to change things? What would an international solution look like?

SH: Of course there is nothing new in the claim that we have to unite and work together, it's the old motto that there is no communism in one country. When I am speaking about a new internationalism, I speak as someone who was born in Yugoslavia, I speak about and from the experience of a historical achievement of the 20th century which is called the Non-Aligned Movement. Just last year – in 2015 – we were marking the 60th anniversary of the Bandung conference which happened in 1955 when the Indonesian president Sukarno invited Yugoslavia's president Josip Broz Tito, India's president Nehru, Egypt's president Nasser and China's Zhou Enlai, and young Indira Gandhi as well. So you can imagine this "line-up" which gathered in Bandung in 1955. Can you see such world powers gathering today and saying that they do not want to play a role in the war in Syria? It's a bit of a disgrace to the Left that no one really celebrated the 60th anniversary of this event. I think that we should remember this and that we could start building a new Bandung conference or a new Non-Aligned Movement by using the five principles that those people laid out at the time. They were conceptualized by Nehru in his speech in 1954 in Sri Lanka. The first was respect for each other's territorial integrity and sovereignty. The second was mutual non-aggression. Third was mutual non-interference in domestic affairs. Fourth was equality and mutual benefit. Fifth was peaceful coexistence.

If you apply these five ideas to our situation today, you can see that none of these applied when it came to Greece, for example. There was no respect of the integrity and sovereignty of Greece, there was a big interference in domestic affairs from the international central banks and private banks and from the media. There was also no peaceful coexistence and there was no respect for mutual benefit. What happened at the Bandung conference was that nations faced with this kind of problem decided to create the Non-Aligned Movement to respond to precisely these things.

Let me use a joke to illustrate this point. It's an old communist joke in which a listener calls Radio Yerevan and asks "Which tea is better, Chinese or Soviet?" The answer is: "Don't get mixed up in a confrontation between super powers, drink coffee." This is precisely the philosophy of the Non-Aligned Movement: in the Cold War we had Soviet Russia on one hand and the US on the other, and the solution was not that we should join one or the other bloc but that we need to oppose both. The same is true of the Brexit question today: the solution is not for Britain to leave the European Union, nor to stay in the current Eurozone, but to oppose both, and to drink coffee, which means to create a possibility on an international level which would oppose both. We can only respond to this crisis by working on an international solution. If the Syrian crisis is something international with more than 20 international players and wide geo-political and geo-strategical and economical causes then the solution to the refugee crisis cannot be found individually or nationally but only internationally. The solution of the refugee crisis is not to invest six billion euros into "outsourcing" the refugee crisis back to Turkey; the solution is not to make Merkel's wonderful gesture and invite one million people to Germany; the solution is also not (though this is needed) for ordinary people to show solidarity in the sense that they take food and blankets and travel hundreds of miles to help; the solution is also not to build walls in Hungary or between Slovenia and Croatia. I could go on. The solution is to come to the core, to the very beginning of the problem, which is the Syrian crisis. If you want to solve the refugee crisis, you have to solve the Syrian crisis, and if you want to do this, there is no way we can do it on a local or national level: it must be international. Of course you can claim that we already have the UN etc., who should be doing precisely this, but the UN is clearly not doing its job here and this is what the Left needs to respond to.

An attempt made by the Left to respond to this problem was the World Social Forum. At the start the World Social Forum had a good paradigm to achieving this because it involved movements from all over the world, from Via Campesina to trade unions from India, and for once there were direct connections between different progressive forces from all continents, a kind of Non-Aligned Movement for the 21st century. But there were problems within the World Social Forum as well and eventually it lost some of its potential and power. For instance, I remember very well, when during the WSF in Senegal 2011 the members of the International Committee of the WSF decided that the WSF could not support officially (as the WSF) the revolution in Egypt – by sending a letter signed by the WSF – because there were so many movements involved and not everyone agreed on all the points. So this was the beginning of the end for the World Social Forum (not to mention that it was sponsored, that year in Senegal, by the biggest oil company in Brazil – Petrobras). An internationalism inside the World Social Forum started to break up at this point and it was the end for its internationalism, so we need precisely a new movement that could go over this fear and be able to say clearly and collectively without fear, with a strong position: "No, we do not want the war in Syria anymore," or, for instance: "Yes, we support Nuit Debout."

AB: So, since we're onto the refugee crisis – before I ask you about "horizontality" and your framework for how this international movement or body might operate – just recently in an article for *Eutopia Magazine* you argued that "Solidarity" actions are, without any doubt, the only morally proper thing to do, but at the same time you say that they actually prolong the refugee crisis. You said something similar just now: that the help of ordinary people is not solving the crisis. You just explained how such actions of solidarity are by no means enough, and how they fail to get to the actual root cause of the issue. But why do solidarity actions prolong the refugee crisis?[9]

SH: When the refugee crisis started, these huge waves of refugees started to come through the so-called Balkans Route, from Greece via Macedonia and Bulgaria, through Serbia, Croatia and Slovenia, then through Hungary (until they built a wall) and then to Austria and finally Germany. My spontaneous reaction was to go to the central stations where two or three trains were arriving every day at the border from Serbia to Croatia. These people were getting out of the trains with no idea at all of what to do; they had all been escaping bloody wars and came on boats through the Mediterranean, then Turkey and Greece, and were really very lost. Many had lost family members, even children, and often everything they owned. The latest statistics show that as many as ten thousand children have been "lost" while the Balkan route was still opened until the end of 2015. No one knows where or how exactly they have been "lost": we can imagine that they drowned or were sold to prostitution or sold for organs and so on, but in any case they have been lost along this long path. So when they arrived in Zagreb, honest people were trying their best to help and my reaction was the same: my reaction was to go there to help. I just went to a supermarket to buy a lot of food. Other people organized themselves to drive as many families as possible for free to help move families because taxis were trying earn money by cheating them by charging five hundred euros to drive half an hour just to take them a short distance to the border. So yes, we need such gestures of solidarity and such gestures actually give me hope. But solidarity, unfortunately, won't solve the problem. What we have to do is to understand and change the structural preconditions which, in the first place, make it possible that a refugee crisis exists at all.

AB: Actually it connects quite well to the question of how to solve things. You've written that after 2011 what you call "horizontality" (which is related to the concept of "direct democracy") must be criticized and overcome, clearly and unambiguously.[10] What are "horizontality" and "verticality" and how are these two concepts going to help us to overcome where we are at?

SH: We still need "horizontality," but it is not enough. Back in 2009 in Croatia, which was before the Occupy movement, I was personally involved in the occupations of faculties, namely the occupation of the Faculty of Philosophy in Zagreb where we occupied the building of the faculty for one month. And each and every day we had something which we called "*plenum*," a classical Yugoslav term, which was actually an anticipation of something the Occupy movement would call a "general assembly." So each day during one month, during the siege, it was really a siege of the whole faculty. The complete University of Zagreb was blocked in a way. We had direct confrontations with the Minster of Education everyday on TV. So, it was really a sort of siege and a sort of commune, because we were sleeping at the faculty. And – it wasn't enough. However, horizontality and direct democracy – and this is important – is a step further from classical protest. When you have a protest you go on the street, you have barricades or you burn something, or whatever. Or you gather in front of a parliament, but when the concept of direct democracy is born it is something which goes beyond a pure protest, it becomes a new form of political life, a new form of organizing, and it happened in Syntagma, at Puerta del Sol, in Zuccoti Park and, most recently, at Nuit Debout.

So when you have people who are staying for the next day then a logical question appears. If there are more people and they are going into the direction of forming themselves as a political body then the next question is: "Okay how do we organize ourselves now?"

In order to organize ourselves, in order to plan concrete next steps, we have to discuss it together. So how do we discuss it together? In order to discuss it together, and decide what to do, we organize a "*plenum*" or a "general assembly." So, in Zagreb we had general assemblies with one thousand people, people who were not only students. This was in the main hall of the faculty, and we discussed completely transparently each step of our next actions. These discussions would last for at least four to eight hours – well, political work is not a tea party or writing an essay, it requires lots of patience and work. And one thousand people were actively participating. I witnessed the same in Zuccotti Park when I was there during Occupy Wall Street. But, at the same time there is a problem. And the problem is that sometimes you need something we might call "verticality." Why?

Because the biggest strength of direct democracy can at the same time be the biggest enemy of direct democracy. So, for example I remember very well from Zuccotti Park that there was a meaningless and completely unproductive discussion which lasted for one hour or so, while, at the same time, the police was encircling Zuccotti Park. They were threatening the participants with eviction and so on. At the same time you had a much bigger political fight on the national level. This was, you know, how to oppose Obama? Do we construct a new political party? Do we join the electoral process or not? At the same time when you had global resonances all around the world because of Occupy Wall Street, people there were discussing for one hour do we need a trash can for red apples or for green apples? I don't remember what it was precisely, but it was certainly something about garbage and how to divide it. Which is ok, ecology is important, but sometimes there are priorities, especially if the whole occupation is under threat. The positive side of horizontality is that people decide together and it's not a representative who decides like in the classical concept of a political representative in parliamentary democracy who is chosen for four years and then he decides in the name of people, but it is the people who decide. But at one point it can become totally counter-productive, as I tried to illustrate in this little example, and I could give you more. It can become counter-productive because not all people can discuss all the things. You know? This is an obvious point. Not all people are equally trained in economy, not all people are equally trained in law, and so on. This is the reason, of course, why during the Occupy Movement we were forming working groups, which are specialized in particular questions. When you encounter a problem, whether it's trash cans or the legal situation of, for example, protesters who were in prison during the protest on Brooklyn Bridge, for example, which happened during Occupy Wall Street, someone has to deal with their legal situation. So we realize that the thousands of us who were in a square, or a hall, cannot solve this question. So what do we do? We construct working groups. It's something that happened already 2009 in Zagreb and it is what also happened in Occupy Wall Street. So you construct working groups, and particular working groups are working with particular problems. So you have a working group on law. You have a working group on media. You have a working group on solidarity kitchen. You have a group on medicine and so on. Then it is the working groups who present the problem and possible solutions for the problem to the general assembly or *plenum*. I think when this process starts to happen you are already starting to combine "horizontality" and "verticality."

In what sense? It doesn't necessarily have to mean that you are going in the direction of representative democracy where you have so-called "specialists" who are dealing with a particular question, but you are building a special kind of organism which is, of course, very... it is very labile. It's an organism that is very fluid, and an organism that is very strong at the same time. But in order for this organism to be strong I think you have to involve "verticality." What I mean by "verticality," to be brutality explicit, I'm thinking about the organizational model of a political party.

AB: So you need to have both horizontality and verticality – the political party and the working groups?

SH: I don't think you have to start by making a protest and then after the protest you start constructing a "horizontal" situation. And then, by constructing this situation you construct general assemblies, you construct working groups, and you construct a new political subjectivity. And once you construct this new political subjectivity the only way to go a step further is to create a political party. No. I'm not saying this.

I say that each movement, each political subject which reaches this concrete phase of political subjectivity, also reaches the question of asking "In which direction do we go now?" They posed this question at Occupy Wall Street, and I remember these discussions. I had this discussion with Gayatri Chakravorty Spivak at that time who was very supportive of Occupy Wall Street, and she said to me on one occasion directly: "If Occupy Wall Street enters the electoral process it will lose because it will lose the very essence because of which Occupy Wall Street was something different and special, which was horizontality." At the same time I had a discussion with the economist Richard Wolff who was also very supportive of Occupy Wall Street, but he had the complete opposite argument. He said: "If Occupy Wall Street doesn't enter the electoral process, it will lose."

So what happened? In a paradoxical way, both of them were right – and wrong. The problem is, on the one hand, that Occupy Wall Street didn't go in the direction of further developing "horizontality" which would maybe be a way out of the deadlock; and on the other hand it didn't dare to join the political arena of classical politics which we know is dirty and you have lobbies, and you have big banks who decide on the electoral candidates. You have Silicon Valley as we can see now in the examples of Hillary Clinton and Eric Schmidt, who was the CEO of Google and doing Hillary Clinton's digital campaign and so on…

So they didn't further develop horizontality, although of course we must be honest and say that there is still an ethic of Occupy all over the US, as there is in Croatia and Bosnia where we also had *plenums*, a new kind of political subjectivity was certainly created… This is not something which can get lost over night. This experience of really working together with people you don't know, and working together with the same ideals and the same goal, is not completely lost. But, this horizontality wasn't organized further, and on the other hand what happened after Occupy was that those who fought against Obama, lost. Obama got elected again.

I think the solution of this deadlock is not to choose either to stay in horizontality or to join the political arena and transform a momentum into a political party. I think the answer should be "No" to both, but "Yes" to a sort of Dialectics. What we have to create is a Dialectics between "horizontality" and "verticality." The moment when a horizontal movement completely excludes the possibility to act as a political party is the moment when this movement actually either has to go in the direction of further developing horizontality, for example with community organizing and participatory budgeting and so on... Or it radicalizes itself, like in the case of the late Sixties in Germany and Italy, where again you had a strong movement on the streets with public discussions, and then what you had as a result in Italy was the Brigate Rosse and in Germany you had Rote Armee Fraktion. I think this is the second option. Which, as we know, failed.

And the third option, which is the most common option, is that this horizontal movement which started with huge enthusiasm actually ends up dissolving itself. Why? Because it's very difficult to occupy a faculty for one month, and it's very difficult to occupy a park like Zuccotti Park for several months. Because you cannot be a professional activist and live from this, you have a job, you have a family, you have friends, and if you invest all your energies into this... it's difficult. So, this is one of the problems of horizontality. On the other hand, if you form a political party, the moment the political party stops to listen to the very people who built the political party you will either end up in a Stalinist concept of a party with purges, where no one is true enough to the goal of the party; or you will end up in the classical example of political parties which we have all around the world, and which are best exemplified, for instance, by the defeat of social democrats all around Europe. So you start with very radical positions but in the end you end up as a typical social democrat, or you don't even end up as a social democrat. So you start as a radical-left party, but in the end you say: "Ah, but we need some compromise."

That's what happened with the British Labor party, you know. You start with a radical agenda and then during Blair it ended up as the worst nightmare with more deregulation of labor, more labor laws, with more so-called "humanitarian interventions" and so on. But what happened then? And that's very interesting in light of the Corbyn experience. I mean we still have to see where it will go, but with Corbyn's success you actually have a different model now, which is the possibility of reforming existing political parties.

You have three models, I would say. One model is Syriza, where you have a political party which was born out of a broad coalition which consisted of different factions, of a spectrum of different political positions. So Syriza is the model of a coalition which was to a certain degree influenced by the movements in the squares. Then you have Podemos, which on the one hand is influenced by the movement in the squares, the Indignados, but on the other hand it wouldn't be possible to build Podemos without having a very smart and wise media strategy. But, again, it wasn't a coalition. And then you have a third model, you have an existing party like Labor. I would never expect it, actually. I mean if I look at my country, at Croatia, or if I look at Germany... can you imagine that the SPD, for example, could be reformed from the inside? I'm not sure, of course, but what Corbyn showed is that it's possible to fight from inside and to change the situation.

Here we come back to the very beginning of this answer. I don't see that the "natural" progress has to be from protest to Occupy, from Occupy to general assemblies, and then when you reach this limit of horizontality then you have to form a political party. What the Labor experience now shows is that you can go the other way around. So you transform an existing vertical party, but what the Labor Party did just after Corbyn took power is that they created something which is called "Momentum," and the goal of Momentum is to address and involve all the thousands of new members, mainly young members, to link them and make sure to integrate the concept of horizontality in an existing vertical party. So, it's very interesting that you can have both ways, and that both ways actually are not ideal, because it seems like what we should do is actually to reach such an organization – which is really difficult and I'm not sure such an organization ever existed or if it will ever exist – but if you have such an organization where you can have an efficient dialectics between "verticality" and "horizontality" at the same time. So it's not the progress from verticality to horizontality, or it's not a top-down method from verticality to horizontality created within the party, but to make sure you have both at the same time.

And maybe closest to that (I'm not sure because it also failed to some degree and Brazil faces a huge political crisis) was the participatory budgeting in Porto Allegre, where actually you had a situation where first you had a movement, with a very basic idea that the city budget must be transparent and that citizens must have the opportunity to participate in deciding how this budget will be spent. It basically means that it's not the Mayor or any particular political representative on the municipal level who decides if a road will be built in the western part of Porto Allegre, or a shopping center will be built in the southern part of Porto Allegre. What usually happens is that, because of capital interests, for example, in the western part, the businessman will bribe the representative and the Mayor will decide to build a road in the western part rather than a kindergarten. This is something which is also occurring on the national level, and also on the global level, of course. What the people realized in Porto Allegre – and then they created the movement – was that they could create an economy and government, a local authority in the city of Porto Allegre, which is not a small city, which would function on the basis of participatory budgeting. Which still doesn't mean that all the people decide. The people can decide on 30% of the budget. So it means that each month you have general assemblies of the western part of Porto Allegre, or of the southern region of the city, and so on... and then people decide where the next budget will be spent. In the sense that you and I would come together, for example, and you just got a child. I will maybe get a child, or my sister will. My sister is definitely getting a child, these days... and then we have a particular interest. And our particular interest is that, instead of a new shopping center, which we don't need actually, because there are existing shopping centers, we actually say: "No! We need a kindergarten because there are more children in this particular neighborhood."

And since the late Eighties and up until, let's say, 2000 or something like that, this system functioned pretty well. Even so far that, during Lula's government in Brazil, it was starting to be implemented on the regional and national level as well. And today you have municipalities in Portugal, and in different countries across Europe, who are actually experimenting with different forms of participatory budgeting.

But to come back to the question of "horizontality" and "verticality," participatory budgeting wouldn't be created in Brazil if in the first place there wasn't a political party, the Workers' Party of Lula, who actually took the idea of the movement and who canalized the energy of the movement in order to enter the political sphere and to say: "Now this is a measure which we want to implement when we come to power." And at the same time, the political party wouldn't have the political program or broad support if there wasn't the movement from the Eighties. So this is how dialectics functions. But the problem is, of course, that political parties very often end up in compromise.

AB: Talking of compromise. I think it's fair to say that we British are just waiting to see what kind of compromise there will be in the case of Jeremy Corbyn – we know it will happen and we are just waiting to see what it looks like and hoping it is not too bad. You mention there that Thomas Piketty was not anti-capitalist enough or really was not anti-capitalist at all. I wanted to ask you about the Subversive Festival (and therefore about the political and strategical concept of "subversion" generally, which is what we are getting into here). I also want to know about your work with Yanis Varoufakis on DiEM25. Varoufakis gave a talk at it, in Zagreb in 2013, which I was very interested in. I know you started that festival back in 2008, when you were only 25 years old, and you invited him even before he became Greece's Minister of Finance. In his talk Varoufakis talked about the fact that they were basically tasked with saving capitalism when they knew it couldn't be saved. Why did they try to save capitalism when they knew it couldn't be saved?[11] Also: he talked about how it would be idiotic to allow capitalism to collapse at that very moment, that the Left was not ready, and that only the racists and Nazis would benefit if capitalism had collapsed at that point. This seems suspicious to me – do you agree with it? Is it another kind of compromise? Would you say you are more of an anti-capitalist than this, or did you agree that we need to save it, at least for the moment? What about now?

SH: The question of compromise. It's also an old question which is always in the air when it comes to the Left. And, I think it brings us to Rudi Dutschke, one of the leaders of '68 in Germany, not because he did a compromise but because he spoke about the concept of the "long march through the institutions" which, unfortunately, often can end up in compromise. He said: "It's not enough to be an extra-parliamentary faction, or to be a political subject outside the parliament. In order to really change things we have to get our hands dirty." Well, he didn't say that, I'm saying that. In other words, we need to seize power even if we want to get rid of power. And it's very difficult to be part of this political game without getting your hands dirty. There are no "beautiful souls." Compromise is always lurking around the corner, but that's precisely why I think that the concept of subversion is of so much importance.

I don't believe that there is something, anything, "outside" of capitalism. At least not today. Maybe on the moon. But not even there. Even Heaven is a battlefield of capitalism. In the Middle Age you had to pay in order to repay your sins and end up in Heaven. I'm completely opposed to this naïve idea that you could get out of capitalism. Like John Zerzan for example, or the Unabomber. This idea that if we attack technology we can, by destroying technology, arrive in some paradise where there is no exploitation and no domination.

But let me just continue with subversion. If it's not possible to get outside of capitalism – if it's not possible to get outside of this box – so the solution is you create a capsule, or a cupola. For example, you have a child, and a stable job, and you decide: "Well the system is fucked up, but I've got a child…" So, I can try to create a capsule for my wife, my child and maybe a close circle of my friends and we can try to live in the capsule, although I know that outside of the capsule there are many other people who also have children and have the same basic need to protect their children, but they suffer. So although we know that there are people outside with the same basic needs, you still close yourself into a capsule because the system is so awful that you know that if you do not, your family will be in danger. So we create this world and we make ourselves think that we cannot change anything because if we do then there is a danger that my capsule will dissolve, or something from the outside world will penetrate the capsule. This is, I think, the reason why a lot of people do not participate in social movements and politics and so on, because they feel it is much safer to stay in this safety net which they are creating each day. And, to be clear on that, I don't want to blame them. We can't blame them.

To give another example of the same point: when we had big protests and *plenums* in Sarajevo two years ago, people were protesting on the streets, thousands of them, burning the institutions of the government etc. It was one of the first massive protests in Bosnia after the collapse of Yugoslavia, really remarkable. More than several thousand people gathered every day, but then, suddenly, people stopped gathering in the streets together. Why did this happen? One explanation – at least from people who come from Bosnia – is that Sarajevo is a small city, not like London or New York, not even like Vienna or Berlin, much smaller. So when the people all gathered, they knew each other. And police knew them as well. After two or three days, an employer comes to a pensioner who was there protesting and said "You know, I have seen that your son was at the protest, and if you do not speak with him, he will lose his job in two days." So, when you have this system where everyone can be blackmailed all the time, you can see why we do not have more social protests. And Sarajevo is just an illustration. We are all so deeply involved within the system via our salaries, indebtment, current jobs, future jobs, that most of the people don't want to take a risk. But today we need risk more than ever. We need subversion.

What is subversion, what does it mean? It means not to attack the system directly – this is a big naivety – terrorists, whether they are left terrorists or Islamic terrorists, always try again and again to attack the system directly. As you can see after the Red Army Brigade (so-called "Baader-Meinhof Complex"), after 9/11 and now again after the terrorist attacks in 2015 and 2016 in Brussels and Paris, the situation becomes even worse than it was before. So for example the German surveillance state was at its strongest during the years of the Red Army Brigade, the so-called "German Autumn." The surveillance period, as exposed by

Edward Snowden, was much bigger after 9/11 than it was before and the society of control in Europe is already much greater after the Paris attacks of 2015. What this shows is that this terrorism does not work or is not capable of overthrowing the system because the system is so strong and it only leads to strengthening it further. This is why the CIA for example had John Brennan criticize Snowden and whistleblowers for exposing NSA secrets, and at the same time the former CIA director James Woolsey was even more explicit and said that Snowden has "blood on his hands." He even said that Snowden should be hanged for what happened in Paris. So we can imagine that an organization like WikiLeaks might be called a terrorist organization very soon – actually the Grand Jury in the US already defines Julian Assange as a "terrorist." What we can see here again is that the system creates an even stronger opposition to the things that oppose it, so again we see that terrorism does not work.

So my answer is subversion. Speaking about the RAF (Rote Armee Fraktion), in the first year of the Subversive Festival I invited Karl-Heinz Dellwo, who has become a great friend since then, who was a RAF terrorist. And he gave a beautiful answer as to what subversion really concretely means. Dellwo was 23 years old when he was part of the squatting movement in Hamburg and he ended up in prison. There, the police beat him and all sorts of things you can imagine and when he came out he realized, of course, that there was really something wrong with the system. At this time there was the first generation of the RAF such as Andreas Baader, Gudrun Ensslin, Ulrike Meinhof and others, who would very soon end up in prison themselves because of their terrorist acts. They were opposing the fact that Nazis were still part of the German government and the Vietnam War and capitalism of course. Dellwo was released from prison and around that time Holger Meins died of hunger strike, who was also part of the first generation of the RAF, and he became the symbol of "Germany in Autumn" (Deutschland im Herbst) at this time. So Dellwo and some friends called themselves the Holger Meins Commando and they decided to try to get into the German embassy in Stockholm. They occupied the embassy, there was a hostage crisis and some people died. Dellwo ended up in prison for 20 years at the age of 23, the first five years of which were in solitary confinement where he saw no one at all. This was a systematic method of the system and it also led to the suicides of Meinhof, Baader and Ensslin who killed themselves because of all these methods of the prison system. After 20 years in prison, Dellwo got out in the beginning of the 1990s and he said that he – although he doesn't justify the violent methods – was not ashamed of what he did; that he would do the same again because he could not live in such a system which was throwing bombs on Vietnam, inviting the Shah from Iran to Berlin, etc.

So, to cut a long story short, in 2008 Dellwo came to the Subversive Festival in Zagreb and there was someone who stood up in the audience and asked him the question: "What does subversion mean? What would the young Dellwo say to the old Dellwo who is sitting on stage at the Subversive Festival which was sponsored by Deutsche Telekom?" Dellwo gave, I think, the best possible answer, he said "Okay, can you tell me which telephone operator you are using? Is it Deutsche Telekom or another one, which is outside of the system do you think?" Then he added jokingly but with a serious point: "When I was young, we had to rob the banks, but now the banks are giving us money." Of course you can say that this is compromise. Okay so we won't take money from Gaddafi, but why not take money from Deutsche Telekom? But wait. In 2013 at the Subversive Festival – which was the year with guests such as Alexis Tsipras, Varoufakis and Žižek, all the "usual suspects" – also Oliver Stone, the Hollywood director, visited us. That year we didn't have Deutsche Telekom but we had Peugeot as one of the sponsors. That year was the biggest; we had an audience of five or ten thousand people there over two weeks, over 200 official guests, hundreds of airport transfers, huge organization. We tried to accommodate all these people and be a professional organizing team. So, there was a press conference with Oliver Stone. There were around 50 journalists in a cinema and some very "subversive" journalist asked the same question – and of course we need to ask questions like this – she asked Oliver Stone: "Is this festival really subversive if it is sponsored by Peugeot?" And Oliver Stone said: "You know, I come from Hollywood and if you want to shoot a movie in Hollywood you need infrastructure, cars, cameras and so on." The journalist was shocked by the answer and, I think, especially by the honesty of it. I think these answers show what subversion can mean. If you want to take power, if you want to overthrow a government, if you want to make a protest or even if you want to go on a date and "occupy" the heart of someone you like – you need infrastructure, technology and the physical means to achieve this. So, for me, the more infrastructure and the greater means that we have, the more chance we have of getting close to our goals. One brilliant text which helps us to see this is *The Anarchist Banker* by Fernando Pessoa, not a very well-known text. Have you heard of that?

AB: I haven't, what is that text about?

SH: It's brilliant. In the midst of hyperinflation in Spain, just before the big global depression, Pessoa writes this wonderful paradoxical text where a young banker comes to a much richer and older banker and he asks the richer banker who is sitting there and relaxing with a cigarette: "I heard from someone that you were an anarchist?" The old banker says: "I am still an anarchist." And the young guy looks at him, this fat banker with an expensive suit smoking on top of a pile of money, and he says: "How can you be an anarchist if you are a banker?" And here I think the real genius of Fernando Pessoa comes and it brings us directly to our future strategical tasks. The anarchist banker says something like this: "When I was young, as you are now, I was an anarchist. We were reading radical literature and throwing Molotov cocktails and we were hoping that without any compromise, we could overthrow the government. But then I asked myself one question, which was this: what is the single thing which has power over all of our lives? I came to the answer: money. So I thought, how can I get rid of the influence of money on our daily lives, how can I get outside of the influence of money? And I realized there is only one way: to have enough money." Of course, my point is not that in order to change capitalism we have to become capitalists, no, but we can't ignore the brutal fact that it is money that is running this system.

We can't, unfortunately, live outside capitalism yet. This is why I am so skeptical of discussions such as Brexit or Grexit – because even if you get out of the EU you have by no means gotten rid of the influence of global capitalism. I am not saying that the Left should become capitalist, but instead we must find various sorts of subversions – like Karl Heinz Dellwo did, who is now running an incredible publishing house in Hamburg, like Oliver Stone did, who recently did a movie on Edward Snowden although no one in the US wanted to financially support the movie, and like Pessoa's anarchist banker did – we have to try to find subversions inside of the system in order to fight the system. Edward Snowden is another figure who managed to show a way to do this and WikiLeaks is another perfect example of what subversion actually means. Here you have an organization that is not a political party and which is also not like the Unabomber or something like that, quite the opposite. This organization is not against technology but is using encryption, using technology, and even when the founder of WikiLeaks, Julian Assange, has been stuck in the Ecuadorian embassy for four years (by 19th June 2016) WikiLeaks didn't stop operating. On the opposite, it became more active than ever. We will talk about this more in the third part of the book on technology, but I think for now I can mention WikiLeaks as another example that gives us a model for subversion, an example that shows how we must use the Machine, the technological infrastructure available to us to subvert, rather than trying to get "outside".

AB: I want to ask about something I've read in your work that might be considered controversial. I want to ask you about the relationship between an increasingly mobilizing working class on the one hand and the rise of the extreme Right and nationalism on the other. In *What Does Europe Want?* you say that it's no coincidence that the extreme-right party in the Czech Republic is called the Workers' Party. This interested me because we see something of this in the UK as well – the UKIP voter-ship (the farthest-right of the main parties) used to be seen as more wealthy but they then harnessed a lot of young working-class votes and started to gain a lot more influence. This upsets the idea that the working-class uprising would be a positive left or liberal thing. Can you say a bit more about how you see the relationship between the mobilizing working class and right-wing politics?

SH: I completely agree because this is precisely the problem of the Left today. It's not the case that if there is a crisis, automatically the working class will be going into the direction of left or even liberal or even democratic politics. Usually, in fact, it's the opposite. I think Yugoslavia is a very good example. During the Eighties, when the Yugoslav self-management economy was already integrated into the global market, we had a huge wave of workers' strikes across Yugoslavia. There was a huge mobilization of the working class all over the country, but not – as many still believe today – in order to get rid of socialism, but to defend the socialist model of self-management (and

Yugoslavia) from its dissolution. Then in the late Eighties, this movement turns into nationalism and becomes a nationalist agenda, so the mobilization of the working class served as a motor for nationalism.

How is this to be explained? I think it can be an example that explains what is happening all around Europe, and perhaps not only in Europe, because you can even see it in America with Donald Trump and in other countries as well. What we can see is that the crisis of capitalism opens up two opposite directions. One is the mobilization of the working class into the direction of nationalism, which includes creating fear of refugees and promoting a return to the nation-state. The other direction is that of the Left and of a new internationalism. But what we have seen is that this other direction often ends up in an *"Eihnbahnstrasse"* (one-way street) and the question is how to explain this. I think the answer is that the Right is winning precisely because it is much easier to convince the "ordinary people" (if we can say that) or the "working class" that the problems and crises of global capitalism can be solved via a retreat to the nation-state. And the Left, I think, has not found a convincing answer to this – actually part of the Left has even tried to do the same and construct an ideology of retreating to the nation-state.

You can see this in Greece for example where some are still advocating an exit from the EU and the Eurozone, the so-called "Plan B." You could have seen it with the Brexit referendum as well, where part of the radical Left claimed that only by retreating to the nation-state can the Left gain power again and achieve national sovereignty. Although I understand this point, I am very skeptical about it for two reasons. First, we can use again the example of Yugoslavia which had a strong economy, one of the strongest armies and one of the strongest diplomacies in the world, and which was part of the Non-Aligned Movement. So, if such a political and economic power as Yugoslavia tried to avoid being integrated into the global market and it failed, how could

Greece, which is just a tiny country on the periphery of EU, achieve what Yugoslavia, a country with decades of real existing socialism, couldn't? What would be there to prevent the possibility that, for example, Chinese capital or Russian capital (which is already present in Greece anyhow) won't simply become the new master in Greece instead of EU banks and institutions? So this is my first concern: even if you exit the Eurozone, you will not exit the constraints of the global market because there is no outside to capitalism. Second, some still seem to believe that if you have a retreat into the nation-state it will be "Us" who will be in power, that it will be "Us" who will form a left government and it will be "Us" that are in control. But I think this is a very dubious idea because if you look at history you will see that in such times of turbulence where the old system is finished and the new system is not born yet, usually it is the radical Right which wins out. So in the case of Greece, if Syriza did not succeed in reforming and taking over the state institutions even though they were in power with a majority, how could a tiny left party like the Popular Unity who were advocating the EU exit and retreat to the nation-state believe that they could be in power and maintain control over the army and the state and that the radical Right will not win out? My answer to this goes back to what we said before: that only radical internationalism can be the real answer to the nationalism of the far Right or the internationalism of Capital. This doesn't mean that we don't have to fight to seize power in each country, or that we don't have to invent radically different monetary models (Bitcoin, digital currencies, etc.). But this must be combined with a new internationalism.

I also think the Left has the problem of something we might describe as "projectionism." Usually the Left has the problem of the phantasm of the good worker – the idea that the working class is reading Marx on the assembly line and at work. And there is a parallel here that some see the refugees as a potentially revolutionary subject. I think this is also a trap. In order to create a revolutionary class out of the refugees we need organization and we need time: it cannot be achieved overnight. The reason that the Right is winning here is because they are operating on the ground. The best example here is the Muslim Brotherhood in Egypt. How can the emergence of the Muslim Brotherhood be explained, after the Arab Spring, after Tahrir? It can be explained precisely by the decades of work in which the representatives of the Brotherhood were on the terrain doing things, although they were banned by the Mubarak regime. They were the ones operating on the ground. To put it in concrete terms, when people needed medicine and food across Egypt in all the villages, it was the Muslim Brotherhood who were providing it. It could be compared with what the Black Panthers did or with what Zapatistas are doing in Mexico, or even with ISIS. To be clear, I am speaking about organizational models here and the relationship between a movement and the people, between an organization and its supporters. The option which young Muslims – once an American drone kills their parents, for instance – have in Syria or Pakistan today is not to join the radical Left because the radical Left (except in Kurdistan) is not really organized. They also don't have the option to join the so-called liberating forces of the US or Turkey. The only option they have, unfortunately, is to join ISIS because they are the only people providing the infrastructure for those people to survive. I think it is precisely here that the Left has failed, perhaps just with one or two exceptions.

AB: So you say that the Left has not yet found a solution to offer an alternative to the Right's ability to use nationalism and the nation-state to gain support, and I think that's quite right. So the question is what needs to be done in order for the radical Left to benefit from the situation of transition and crisis that we are in, instead of the radical Right? Do you think this kind of international solution – the alternative to a nation-state

solution – should also construct itself as an ideology, so that people have something to believe in other than a nation-state, in order to produce a kind of pan-Europe solution?

SH: Absolutely, and I think here we approach a problem that was described by Benedict Anderson in his well-known book *Imagined Communities*, where he showed how the concept of the nation-state was born. So what to do in times of "fluid identities" and in a situation in which you do not have fixed co-ordinates anymore because of the crisis provoked by financialization? What we should do in order to create a new internationalism is first to deconstruct the idea of "nation"; and second we should try, precisely by deconstructing the very possibility of something like the nation and national sovereignty, to show that the whole situation has changed and that today we are in a situation where there is no such thing as national sovereignty and it can never be regained. This is because there are no borders for capitalism, for trade and secret agreements like TTIP, TISA or TTP. There is no way to fight against these using the idea of national sovereignty. Take for example, Phillip Morris suing the state of Australia or multinational companies suing the states of Ecuador or Russia. All these examples show that corporations are stronger than the state and that therefore there is no other solution but an international one.

Interview Two: Love

Alfie Bown: So we are moving now onto the second of our three topics here. Before we get on to the serious material discussed in your book *The Radicality of Love*,[12] which contains questions of the relationship between love, politics and revolution, let me start things off with a fun question. The question is this: what do you think of Tindr, Grindr and online dating?

Srećko Horvat: Right – so I think that Grindr, Tindr and online dating are perfect illustrations (and also sad illustrations) of where we are at the moment when we speak about love. Recently when I was in London I was reading the usual newspapers circulating such as the *Evening Standard* and the *Metro* and I saw this title: "Outsource your online life with a Cyber-Butler." This is the newest trend and it's very interesting to follow these trends, because they also give us theoretical answers to what is happening with love in the 21st century. So this service advertised in the newspaper works by setting up your dating profile on all the sites so that you no longer need to go on the dating websites. All you actually need to do is turn up at the right time and place to have the date that has been organized for you. The ideology behind this is that it's the perfect service for a busy professional who doesn't want to waste time doing all that is necessary to fall in love, so they "outsource" it. So just like Apple is outsourcing the production of iPhone to Foxconn in Taiwan who is then outsourcing to China, what you have now is a transition of this capitalist model into the most intimate sphere: into the sphere of dating.

So what you have with this new service is that someone else does everything instead of you and all you have to do is turn up in the restaurant and there you have the date. You can see the problem immediately: in order to have an encounter with someone, it is not enough for your Cyber-Butler to sort out all the preconditions and then you will fall in love. However, a new problem we have here is that a machine might actually be able to find an ideal match for you using all the characteristics and preferences that you have. You can give a search engine the parameters of everything you like, which is already what online dating does and which is now happening more and more, so you give certain parameters: the music I like, the food I like, my religious views, political preferences and of course my sexual preferences. And these parameters are getting more and more precise in the very recent past and also other people's parameters are getting more and more precise so that you can now genuinely imagine that an artificial machine or artificial intelligence might soon be able to predict your ideal date better than you can yourself.

This is precisely the story of the movie by Alex Garland, *Ex Machina* (2015). The story of the movie goes like this: you have a big search engine similar to Google, and this machine predicts our desires according to the searches we do every day online where we live our most intimate desires and dreams. So a guy who is the experimental rabbit in the film, like in a Turing test, has to test to see if the AI is really AI, and falls in love with this very cute girl, who is actually a robot who is very clever and who can re-create emotions very well. At the end of the movie the owner of the search engine reveals that he created this AI machine in order to make him fall in love with her. Using his search history and all his preferences, this fictional Google has determined exactly what he will fall in love with. Actually, the very appearance of the AI girl was based on the boy's pornography searches.

I think it's fair to say that we have not yet reached this situation, but what the newest trends in online dating show is that we are going towards this dystopian world of science fiction where falling in love will be "outsourced," even if we are not quite there yet. What they show – and here we come to a more theoretical and psychoanalytic point – is that falling in love basically, in its essence, is constituted by the same kind of mechanisms. So even the myth of falling in love on first sight is already pre-conditioned, even if it appears to be free and not mediated. Even this classical idea of unmediated love has this kind of structure inside of it which is basically, I think, a narcissistic structure.

AB: To stay with *Ex Machina*, is the horror of the film that he believes that this is true love and then realizes that it is in fact formulaic and structured by technology? So we are thinking of things which appear totally your own and personal but are in fact formulaic and structured? Is love something like this?

SH: The French psychoanalyst Jacques Lacan claims that falling in love is when the "Ego falls in love with the Ego itself on the imaginary level." This is exactly what happens in *Ex Machina*, and another even better example is Spike Jonze's *Her* (2013), in which Joaquin Phoenix falls in love with an operating system which has the voice of Scarlett Johansson. But in fact, all he is falling in love with is himself (that's why a more appropriate title of the film would have been *Him*), so what I think is shown to us here is that very often we are falling in love not with the other person but with ourselves so that you don't even need the other, you just need the image of yourself in the eyes of the other. Of course, another parallel is the classical story in the third book of *Metamorphoses*, the story of Narcissus, where the subject loves in the other the image that it would like to inhabit itself.

You can see this, for instance, when you start to fall in love and you start writing love letters. When people write love letters – in most of the cases, I am afraid – they are not writing to the beloved but instead they are writing to themselves. What we have in the love letter is the voice of this new subjectivity of our own that we are constructing for ourselves in writing. I can give you an example. Recently Julian Assange told me about all the love letters that he has received since he is entrapped in the Ecuadorian embassy in London. Most of these letters – and I have only seen one big box of them – have the same structure. These people are real admirers of Assange, but they are also people who have fallen in love with him because he is the symbol of Western dissidence, a hacker who has really succeeded in opposing the most powerful Western power. I think we could go so far to claim that these people have not really fallen in love with him but with the idea that they have fallen in love with the opponent of Western power who is arbitrarily detained in the Ecuadorian embassy, and they have actually fallen in love with the idea that this person could fall in love with them. So it's actually a scenario from an espionage movie and they have fallen in love with this idea.

It is also like the first scene in Goethe's *Sorrows of Young Werther*, where Werther falls in love with Lotte. When does that particular moment occur? It is a scene where Lotte is cuddling children and it is an archetypal scene in which the image of his mother is re-created. What it means is that even before love at first sight, there is already always the construction of a narrative, even if we are not aware of it. So this is what I really want to say, that there is no falling in love without a narrative and I would even call it a "narrative contract." The whole story behind *1001 Nights*, the classic Arab story, is based on a narrative contract. Scheherazade gives a narrative per day to have her life prolonged for one day each time. We see the same thing again in Lars von Trier's movie *Nymphomaniac* (2013) where Charlotte Gainsbourg gives Stellan Starsgaard a narrative at each moment in order to keep going so that he prolongs her life. I think what these movies – *Nymphomaniac*, *Ex Machina* and *Her* – show us is that a basic mechanism of falling in love is narcissism, that narcissism lies at the very core of the process of falling in love, we always already at the same time also fall in love with ourselves. This is not the same as what I mean by the "radicality of love" or "radical" love.

AB: It strikes me how Lacanian these two movies *Ex Machina* and *Her* are. Especially the fact that in *Ex Machina* the object of his every desire ends up killing him or leaving him to die, so that the achievement of your deepest desire destroys you.

SH: You have the same thing in *Her*! Here AI means that she can be in love with thousands of people at the same time, which happens at the very end of the movie once her operating system is so advanced that she can multitask (be in various relationships at the same time) at incredible speed. Let us go a step further here: wouldn't true love appear if Joaquin Phoenix accepted her for what she is – AI – and that she can be with 60 thousand different partners at the same time?

AB: Two last things on this topic. Can you say something about your idea of "masturdating"? And also – how modern is this idea? Did you ever have a Tamagotchi?

SH: I did not, but my friends did – it was highly popular in the Nineties.

AB: Is the Tamagotchi the start of a trajectory of feeling towards machines which culminates with *Her* and *Ex Machina*?

SH: I completely agree that all these trends – the "outsourcing" of dating, these films and the Tamagotchi, and then of course the newest trend of "masturdating" – are all part of a new paradigm. For instance, what the Israeli sociologist Eva Illouz shows in her books is that even romance, which is part of the paradigm of "romantic love," is becoming part of a new culture of narcissism.

Romantic love is based on the idea of "romantic atmosphere" and even small children already know how to recognize or to conceptualize a romantic atmosphere. If you ask them what is "romance," they will – as a recent study showed – answer that "romance" is going to an expensive dinner with a candle and similar stuff in which you can recognize a pattern of commodification and rationalization which has nothing to do with a genuine feeling. And again, something which is perceived to be part of our personal and intimate sphere, the most spontaneous and emotional part of our life, is actually constructed and part of a historical development – note how "expensive dinner" is perceived as being something "romantic"; it is as if "the more you pay, the more you care" – at least lots of people believe and practice that.

But that said – what we are approaching nowadays, I think, is a change in this paradigm or a new paradigm which was already described by Christopher Lasch in his book *The Culture of Narcissism* (which was published in 1977) and later in his book *The Minimal Self* (which was published in 1984), which showed that actually the pathological narcissism in 20th-century American culture was in a way the creation of the radical Left and of the period of '68. In what sense is this the case? He said that "after the political turmoil of the 60s, Americans have retreated into purely personal preoccupations. Having no hope of improving their lives in any of the ways that matter, people have convinced themselves that what matters is physical self-improvement: getting in touch with their feelings, eating healthy food, taking lessons in ballet and belly dancing, immersing themselves in the wisdom of the east and overcoming the fear of pleasure."[13] This is Lasch's analysis from the late Seventies. What we have had in the meantime is the development of technology and what I think is most important is that with technology you do not even need the other anymore, you can satisfy your every desire without it.

Unfortunately, very few sociologists or philosophers today tackle the problem of technology. On the other hand most people who work on technology are not interested in feelings and emotions. So this makes me want to think about how love is affected technologically and I can now come to the concept of "masturdating" that you asked me about, a concept which reaches back, I think, just to 2015. Again it comes from an article I encountered in the British newspaper *Metro*, which said that going alone to a dinner or an art gallery is actually more quality time than going on a date. This is why it is called "masturdating," which comes, of course, from "masturbating" and "dating": dating alone. So I think we have really approached a sad and tragic era from which there may be no turning back, if people have to be taught how to be alone. To really be satisfied when you are alone, to be a complete person when you are alone and not searching for the "other half" is, I think, a precondition for any true radical love. But what people have lost, and what trends like "masturdating" and "solo weddings" (which exist now in Japan, where you can actually go and have a marriage and wedding with yourself) show is precisely a lack of solitude. I don't think these things are teaching us how to be alone, to reach real solitude, but instead they are showing what Lasch claimed in the Seventies: that this is narcissism. I think, to be truly alone, even in this kind of existential anxiety where there are no fixed coordinates around you, I think this is the real condition for any true radical love to emerge.

AB: So let's briefly loop back to "polyamory" which is another circulating and popular idea of many loves or many partners. Do you see this as radical love?

SH: To answer the question let me use the title of one of Woody Allen's movies, which is *Whatever Works*. The basic idea of polyamory is that at one time you can love many people and I think this is true, you can. But that takes a lot of time, which is why I am not into these kinds of things myself because I do not have time and I would have even less time if I was polyamorous. I am not at the level of Scarlett Johansson in *Her* where she can have thousands of loves at once: she can do it because she is artificial intelligence. The other problem is something I have seen with many friends who are polyamorous. The problems start when not all stake-holders (let's call them like that) are aware that they are in polyamory. So to have real polyamory all subjects involved would need to agree that they are in such a relationship and then it can be four people, ten people or whatever. So what I have attempted to show in my book *The Radicality of Love* is that even in polyamorous relationships very similar problems to those which exist in classical relationships start to appear so that they end up with jealousy, private ownership and even nuclear family structures. If you look at the development of communes in Austria or in the US during '68, you will see that all these really radical experiments in the realm of the most intimate sphere, that of love, ended up in all the same classical problems once more. So I think that if we are going to redefine love we need something much more than polyamory.

AB: Right, so we can get into the main argument of your book here. We have touched upon the idea of love or falling in love as a totally conformist thing, something that can be institutional, organized and conservative. But you are after a radical love – or a love which is a kind of revolutionary thing? I came to your book with Alain Badiou's little book, *In Praise of Love*, in mind and perhaps also Derrida.[14] My understanding of the argument there is that love is or can be transformative – a Badiouan event – and maybe you are saying that therefore it has the power to be transformative in a political sense as well? Would that be right? Is there a difference between yourself and Badiou?

SH: First of all – I don't completely agree – I don't think that falling in love is conservative as such (though it can be). It can be a radical and violent thing that can change your life. But what I am claiming is that falling in love already contains, as an intrinsic value, mechanisms of narcissisms in itself and something that is not radical at all. So I would say that falling in love can be what Badiou calls an event. But to go on in Badiou's terms, what you need after the fall (and here I agree with Badiou, though I disagree when it comes to love and politics), what you need after the fall is fidelity. It doesn't mean that you cannot end up with other partners after you find the one partner (so polyamory can function). Fidelity means something more: that even if you end up with another partner you are able to reconstruct and reinvent your love again, so that this doesn't become a victim of your own narcissism again. Fidelity means that you stay true to the first basic event which can be deciding that this is the person with whom I want to spend the rest of my life because this person understands me and I understand this person the most out of everyone, but it also means something else: what Badiou calls the love of difference and not the love of identity.

For me this means that love can be an affirmative desire towards the other which means to respect the other and not to destroy the otherness of the other. What you have in the idea of romantic love has its origin in the idea of the missing half or the concept of "soul-mates." It's the old myth present in Plato's *Symposium* where one part is trying to find the other complimentary part and as long as it doesn't find this missing part it will never be complete. What we need to rehabilitate today is precisely the opposite. If anything has been taught to us by psychoanalysis it is that each of us has a certain lack and that the other is not someone who is able to compensate this lack, which is the reason why Lacan says that "Love is to give something that someone doesn't have... to someone who doesn't want it." This should be the basic formula of the "radicality of love," which would mean accepting the very difference of the other, to accept the otherness of the other, and I think that this could be a way out of the current problem where people are trapped in narcissism and cannot get out of it.

AB: So can we outline the difference between yourself and Badiou more clearly?

SH: The main point that Badiou makes in *In Praise of Love* is that politics and love are opposed to each other. For him, politics is centered around the collective, and love around individuals and excludes the political. So Badiou says that love is part of an individual project, though he is also sometimes contradictory – as when he says that love is a communism for two – which implies collectivity. I think people are often mixing "falling in love" with love itself, and even Badiou does it as well sometimes. When Badiou talks about love as opposed to politics: if we exchange the word love for "falling in love," I would then agree with him. If you take the classic examples of "falling in love" from classical literature to modern movies, "falling in love" is always based on isolation and it's based on excluding the collective. Here I would agree with Badiou if we talk about "falling in love" – we can see it in the sexual triangle in Bernardo Bertolucci's *Dreamers* (2003). In this film we are in 1968 in an apartment and Molotov cocktails are going off on the streets but the characters are just inside a Parisian apartment excluded from the collective action and experimenting with sex. But this is "falling in love" and not radical love.

What I tried to develop in *The Radicality of Love* is to show that it *is* possible, in a way, to unite politics and love. I would even go so far as to say unlike Badiou that *love is politics* and that if we wanted to avoid the biggest horrors of the 20th century then we need love. It doesn't mean that I want to go into the naive hippie direction or into the direction of communes, but that we should redefine love itself. Lenin for example had the same problem as Badiou. He was opposed to love because he was convinced the energy "invested" into love should be invested into revolution. This is best embodied in the famous Maxim Gorky anecdote about Lenin who couldn't listen to Beethoven's "Appassionata" anymore because instead of smashing people's heads it gives him a desire to "say gentle stupidities and stroke the heads of people who, living in this dirty hell, can create such beauty." I would say that Lenin would agree with Badiou in saying that love is opposed to politics, but I think that history would show that he was wrong and that this can lead, ultimately, to totalitarianism. No wonder Badiou is still a Maoist. On the other hand, someone like Che Guevara would be an example of how love and politics can be combined.

AB: So how does Che Guevara prove this point to us that love and politics can be and should be combined?

SH: I think first I should say that most of what we think about when we say "Che Guevara" is, fortunately or unfortunately, a myth. We mainly talk about an image rather than the person. So what I tried to do was read his writings very closely. I found that in his earlier writings as a young revolutionary there was a divide or at least a tension between love and politics that was very much present. Then he talked about how revolutionaries have to be "killing machines," but then just several years later he writes that revolutionaries have to be driven by a great feeling of love, so there is a contradiction. But what he succeeded in doing in his political and private life is to resolve this tension or contradiction. So I agree with Badiou that there is always an eternal tension between love and politics but I think that this tension can be resolved and that Che Guevara managed to do this.

I think this combination of the two, an overcoming of the tension between love and politics, can create better politics and better love as well. Che Guevara shows that love should be thought of as political rather than as the desire to escape the political field and isolate yourselves. This part of Che Guevara was only revealed ten years ago when Aleida March, his wife, published his memoirs and revealed that he was reciting, for instance, Pablo Neruda when he was in Africa and sending letters back to Cuba. In one letter, one of the most beautiful letters, he wrote: "Love me passionately but with understanding, my path is laid out and nothing but death will stop me." Then he writes that "some journeys we will be able to take together, some not" and then he says, deconstructing the myth of Guevara as a killing machine, that "what drives me has nothing to do with a casual thirst for adventures and what that entails." But on the other hand you can see that he had the same tension. In a letter written in Tanzania in 1965, depressed and sad, Guevara writes to his wife Aleida: "Now that I am a prisoner, with no enemies nearby, or injustices in my sights, my need for you is virulent and physiological, and cannot always be calmed by Karl Marx or Vladimir Ilych." It's interesting to see that even such a person who is the best example of a revolutionary or is the model of a revolutionary, had the same tension between love and politics that Badiou discusses. However, unlike Lenin, who suppressed love and in fact suppressed his love towards Innesa Armand because he had to focus only on investing energy into the revolution, Guevara succeeded in keeping both and in resolving this tension between politics and love. When he visited Aleida and his children undercover as a different man, which was the last visit, he was pursuing the idea of revolution but also the idea of love. I don't want to leave the impression that I see Che Guevara as the answer to Badiou's tension between politics and love but I think he can be a positive example. I think another is one of the biggest feminists of the 20th century, Alexandra Kollontai, who was a minister in Lenin's cabinet. She also shows that politics deals with emotions and emotions can also be political. I think this is the field where we should go in order to construct a better politics and make the world a better place and also in order to develop a better approach to relationships. Following examples like Guevara and Kollantai can be useful here.

AB: We're talking about your main argument that love and politics belong together and not apart, separating you from Badiou's argument. And I'm aware that our interview has the first section on politics and the second on love. It seems that we have a Badiouan structure, where our contents page separates love from politics, whilst we oppose the idea in our conversation. Would it be possible to connect these sections? I mean to use the connection between politics and love to explore the relationship between this conversation and our last one. You just talked about making the world a better place politically, and what we were really talking about in the politics section was how to create a practically useful way forward in Europe. So my question is: can love help in Europe?

SH: Definitely. Again I have to say: not in the sense of the hippie idea of love. The nonsense idea that love can prevent the Vietnam War, the refugee crisis, etc. – this is too simplistic. What I think is that the relationship between love and politics is so important and you can see this clearly if you start from a very basic assumption. If you are in a room with any two people – it can be any two people and any room: a workspace, a dining room, the barricades or a parliament – you are already creating a relationship. This relationship is never only a relationship between friends in the dining room, colleagues at work, politicians in parliament or revolutionaries at the barricades. At the same time it can be a relationship between politicians, it can be a relationship between friends, it can be a relationship between ex-lovers, and – to come back to Carl Schmidt's basic idea of politics – it can be a relationship of enemies.[15] It can be various things all at once. A basic relationship between two or three people already involves desires, emotions and affects.

What most of the political philosophers – except, I would say, Spinoza, Lyotard with his "libidinal economy," Deleuze and Guatarri with their philosophy of desire, and Negri's reading of Spinoza – have not fully taken into consideration is that love and desire are already part of politics. Moreover, there is no politics without desire. What I tried to show in *The Radicality of Love* is that you can see this realization of "libidinal economy" by looking, for example, at totalitarian systems. I did, among other things, not only research on the October Revolution or '68, but also the Iranian Revolution. These political systems try not only to control or suppress, but to create power, as Foucault would have said. What really powerful regimes do is not only prohibit desires and stop us from acting on our desires but create desires as well. This is exactly what the Iranian Revolution did for example, but we could also give other examples: take the French Revolution, in which what we can call modern pornography – which was then still subversive unlike today's pornography! – was created. These revolutionary political movements created desire.

So what I am saying is that we cannot understand modern politics until we understand (or without understanding) these realms of desire and even love. To put it another way, I cannot imagine an occupation (and I have participated in a decent number of occupations from Bosnia to Zuccotti Park) in which there are not these kinds of relationships. So I think to have a successful political party or to have a successful government or to have revolution or to stay in power after the revolution, to do any of these things, I think you need also to know what to do with the emotions and affects of people. What the Nazis or anyone comparable did was manage to change the people and create new intimate spheres. Like we discussed above, Orwell's *1984* is based on the idea that all energy used on love is wasted when it could be used for the Party, which is why in that novel you have something called "The Ministry of Love" and "The Anti-Sex League," who deal precisely with desires. The main aim of each totalitarian and political system, even a liberal social-democratic system, works like this. When Obama said "Yes, we can!" this was a political statement but it was also counting on emotions, and specifically, hope. Did he succeed? Of course, not. What we can see today is that the Right – just take Donald Trump – can appeal to people much more directly and easier precisely because they are aiming at emotions and affects. The same with Brexit: it was not a rational debate at all, it was highly emotional. Again it comes back to our earlier discussion about the Right and the Left. The Right has managed much more to manipulate and use emotions to its advantage than the Left has and if I have one claim about love it is this: that if the politics and political philosophy of the Left is to be successful it must take love seriously again.

AB: Maybe a lot of these discussions are connected here. What we talked about under the heading of "politics" is a solidarity between people without looking for a sameness in the other – a solidarity or collectivity which is not denying otherness and making us all the same as each other. Something which doesn't make us nationalist and the same as each other – but a solidarity which embraces the other's otherness, which matches up with your criteria for "radical love"?

SH: Yes, this is a very good point. If you take the refugee crisis, even solidarity is not enough. What we need to do to solve the refugee crisis is to learn precisely that we *don't* need to love the other. Even if we have refugees, the way to solve it is not try to love them but to acknowledge that I do not love every person because I cannot love every person. Instead I want to embrace the otherness of each person and not do what you said, a very good way of putting it, not insist on the sameness of the other or try to assimilate them into being the same. For me, sameness is the ultimate dystopia.

You have a perfect illustration of the dangers of sameness in a recent movie, one of the best I have seen in the last year. It's a film by the Greek director Yorgos Lanthimos and it's called *Lobster* (2015). *Lobster* is the opposite of Godard's 1965 film *Alphaville*, where the dystopia is a world where emotions are prohibited. In *Alphaville* an IMB-style supercomputer controls people who smile and cry and if they fall into the realm of emotions, they are executed. That was Godard's vision of a future dystopian society: a world in which love and desire are prohibited. This is also the idea of the Iranian Revolution – prohibition.

Why *Lobster* is interesting is that precisely 50 years after Godard, the dystopian future is exactly the opposite: a society in which it is prohibited *not* to be in love. You have, in the film, a hotel, which is on the outskirts of the city. So-called "Loners" go to this hotel, and they have 45 days to find a lover with whom to pair, and if they don't succeed they are turned into an animal of their choice. Only people in relationships can live inside the city so that we have the opposite to *Alphaville*: here it is impossible and prohibited to be alone. A beautiful and unexpected twist in the film happens when the main character escapes to the woods and finds a kind of "resistance" movement which is opposed to the "totalitarianism of love." But wait. Instead of promoting "free will" and freedom, the "loners" are also totalitarians of their own sort: they prohibit love. You can only be alone. So what we see here is the idea that sameness is the ideal – we are all different, but we must be the same, either alone or in love. This is the trap that we need to get out of, the current trap we described right at the beginning of this conversation. And to get out of this trap what we need to do is to detect the traces of the ideology of sameness in love and friendship and get out of the search for sameness, replacing it by moving towards otherness. The virtual world in which we perceive friendship in terms of "likes" or "pokes," or the categories of things that we "like," this world is creating precisely sameness. Grindr and Tindr and also social networks like Facebook, which may seem less dangerous, are all part of this construction of sameness: it is a kind of search for the same. Instead of all this we should look to affirm otherness, not to destroy the otherness of the other but to affirm it. So we come back to what Nietzsche says in his *Zarathustra*: that we have to become "Yes-sayers" – what Heidegger called *Zu-Sage*, those who say "Yes" to the otherness. This is not to transform the other into ourselves or into something which is known, which is still part of narcissism, but to keep the other as something unknown and to love the other precisely for this, to love the "unknown unknowns," to put it Donald Rumsfeld's words.[16]

Interview Three: Technology

Alfie Bown: We've touched upon technology already – specifically on how technology is something that pervades everything, even love, apparently the deepest emotion, which has become inseparable from technological issues. Let's start with a simple question then – why is it technology which is the most important thing to be thinking about in today's society?

Srećko Horvat: Technology has always been one of the most important topics of philosophy since the times of Plato and Aristotle and the question of *techne* and *epistēmē*. I think this was a crucial field of research and also a way to understand the world: without understanding technology we cannot understand the world. If we take into consideration the ancient difference between *techne* and *epistēmē* – where *techne*, as defined by Aristotle, means "craft" or even "art," and *epistēmē* is defined as knowledge – I think what we are reaching in the 21st century is the fact that *techne* has actually become *epistēmē* and that it is now impossible to maintain a division between *techne* and *epistēmē* anymore precisely because of the rapid development of technology. Now, this was already announced by Martin Heidegger in his Bremen lectures in 1949.[17] What he outlined here was very interesting because he also asks us to re-think and re-define the distinction between *techne* and *epistēmē*. What he says in the most important part of his lecture (in the 1940s before the Internet, before Google and so on) is that technology has become a new mode of being and that technology can never be overcome. He says that because of technology all distances in time and space are becoming more narrow. He argues, for instance, that agriculture is now a mechanized food industry and that this is the same as the production of corpses in the concentration camps. He thinks, quite correctly, that if agriculture is a mechanized food industry it is very similar to the concentration camps.

If you fast-forward – and here is the part where I don't agree with Heidegger – in his famous Spiegel interview of 1966 (not published until ten years later after Heidegger's death), when asked by Spiegel about the question of technology, he says that now "Only a God can save us." This is now the classical Heideggerian view that if technology creates a new mode of being which cannot be overcome then we need saving by a god, which means basically that we can't be saved. I think that Heidegger is deeply wrong here. Only 20 years earlier in the Bremen lectures Heidegger had quoted the German poet Freidrich Hölderlin, saying that "Where the danger lies, there also grows that which saves us."[18] It seems interesting and peculiar to me that Heidegger forgot his previous view that technology is based on something that Plato called *pharmacon*. At the same time as it can be a danger, as Hölderlin says, it can also be salvation. At the same time it can be a medicine or a cure. Just take nuclear energy: it can be an atomic bomb or a source of energy. Any kind of technological invention can be used in one direction or it can be used in another.

AB: So for Heidegger, technology transforms the "natural" world into raw materials. For example he says that the Rhine, once "a river in a landscape" becomes "a water power supplier" when the hydroelectric plant is conceived of and built. His argument is that humans are turned into raw materials by technology – is that something you agree with or object to? It seems that with Big Data this is increasingly coming to be true.

SH: Yes, I think that is right, but it is only part of the whole story. What we have with Big Data and the harvesting of information though Facebook and Google, is that humans indeed become raw materials, showing again that with technology we are entering a new mode of being. But what worries me even more is something which is now happening with the Internet. The Internet, which did not exist during Heidegger's time, is one of the biggest creations of humankind. And as we just said, like any technological advancement, it can be both the weapon of mass destruction and the means for a new evolution of humanity. I think what the Internet created is the possibility of something that Pierre Teilhard de Chardin, back in 1922 in his *Cosmogenesis*, called the "Noosphere," a word coming from the Greek word for "mind" (*nous*) and "sphere." He said that with the "Noosphere" what humanity might approach is a new level of consciousness. After the "geosphere" and the "biosphere," he says, the third succession of the development of Earth will be the "Noosphere," which means the sphere of the mind. Here we see that almost 100 years ago, the Internet was anticipated by someone who did not even know what the Internet is. Why? Because it is precisely the Internet that increasingly ties its users together into a single information-processing system that functions as a global "nervous system"; it is what H. G. Wells called the "World Brain." Remember how Marshall McLuhan, in his book *Understanding Media* from 1964, defines the media as an extension of ourselves. This is still the best definition of technology: the wheel is an extension of the leg, the microphone is an extension of our voice and headphones are an extension of our ears. The next stage then is the "Noosphere," because I think the Internet has become the global brain, the nervous system of our global society, the extension of our mind and all senses at the same time. What we had before was particular technologies as described by McLuhan – the wheel, the lighter, the telephone, etc., but with the Internet we have a connection of all of these.

In 1995, which already belongs to an archeology of our recent history that no one remembers anymore, the Internet had only ten million users. In 2011 it already had two billion users and in 2020, according to the latest statistics, it will have more than four billion users – and probably even more. Perhaps by the time this book is published all this will already be part of an archeology of the future as well, because everything changes so rapidly and each new connection creates multiple new combinations. It was already a huge historical achievement when ten million people were connected – but what does it means when we compare it with two billion people in 2011? It doesn't only mean that we can be in contact with someone in Asia, Africa, Europe, etc. It doesn't only mean that you or I can talk with ten different people at the same time although we are not necessarily physically present. It doesn't only mean that you can share a status on Facebook or Twitter and it can be shared by millions of people depending on how popular you are on the social networks. What it actually means is that – and here we come to Google, which I think is the most revolutionary company in human history – what it actually means is that via all these developments and possibilities created by the Internet, we are approaching a new level of consciousness – we can call it "Noosphere" I would even go as far as to say that the Internet and companies like Google and other Silicon Valley startups are creating – and I am not exaggerating here – a new evolution of humankind and of the human mind.

AB: Can you qualify what you mean by saying that Google is the most revolutionary company in the history of the world? People will wonder whether you mean this in a positive or negative way. Can you maybe outline where we need to be wary of the revolutionary qualities of Google, and where we might be looking to embrace, take advantage of and use them in a revolutionary way? Where do Google and Facebook sit in relation to revolution?

SH: When I say that Google is the most revolutionary company in history I say that with *pharmacon* in mind again – that at the same time this is the most dangerous company, but at the same time anyone interested in the power of technology in the world today can see that this is intellectually very exciting as well. What Google is doing is intervening in this idea of what I call the evolution of the human mind. I think that in order to have any possibility of changing the world – and again I am not exaggerating – the only way to change anything is to understand Google. Before the existence of the Internet we were dependent on individual technologies that were slowly connecting the world – the telegram, the telephone and then dial-up internet, etc. – which all arrived in the 20th century. At the end of the 20th century we then saw the rapid acceleration of this into a full hyperconnectivity. What Google did was use this new hyperconnectivity – or more precisely, data integration – to build the most powerful company in the world.

In January 2016, Google became the most highly valued company in the world. In 2010 both Apple and Google were worth less than 200 billion dollars each, but today each is worth over 500 billion dollars. On top of this, Google spends more money on registered political lobbyists in Washington DC than any other company in the world, spending more than any other company in order to influence political decisions, more than any arms companies or anything like that. So at the same time as it became the most valuable company in the world it became very close to the State Department. Those at the top of Google are closely connected with the US State Department. So Jared Cohen, the director of Google Ideas, was advisor to Clinton until 2010. Eric Schmidt is actually now the leader of Hilary Clinton's digital campaign and he became the boss of a special committee at the Pentagon which will deal with the increasing integration between Silicon Valley companies and the US army sector. It is not a surprise that he was Google's CEO and that in his book with Jared Cohen, *The New Digital Age*, he explicitly said that the technology companies will be to the 21st century what arms companies were to the 20th century.

So Google, with their most famous motto, "Don't be Evil," are not a neutral company at all and they are very well connected to the US deep state and this should worry us. All this is the case, but philosophically this is also very exciting to follow because Google – and this is the reason it is the most revolutionary company, not only because it is close to the political power – succeeded by using technological innovation and the very existence of the Internet to create a monopoly that is so extreme that 83% of people in the US use Google, most of them even before they get out of bed in the morning. 83% of people use Google to access the Internet, so that for most of humankind today Google and the Internet mean the same thing.

Why is this relevant from a political perspective? If Google decides to favor one candidate in an election, for instance, we can see that its influence over undecided voters is so great that they can easily have an influence over who wins the election. If you just look at the data – in 2012 in the general election, Google donated more than 800 thousand dollars to Obama and this should really warn us. What these big tech companies are doing more and more is precisely the opposite of Google's most famous logo. So recently, for example, WikiLeaks published Hillary Clinton's emails, which show that Jared Cohen created an online tool for rebels to help bring down the Syrian regime. What you can see here is that Google is not just about technology but is also intervening on a geo-political level, and not just by helping with Clinton's digital campaign. What's more, if you just think about how Google works, you realize that it is Google that determines which webpages appear on your search and how to rank them. 50% of our clicks go to the first two items on the search and 90% go to the ten items on the first page of the results. The same will be true for presidential candidates, for example: Google can decide.

So that is Google. Now, let's come to Facebook. When the Paris terrorist attacks happened in November 2015, Facebook created the so-called "safety button" so that each user could switch on the safety button and let their friends know they are safe. What is wrong with this? I am not going down the classic route of relativization and saying "What about the safety buttons for attacks in Burkina Faso, Beirut or anywhere else?" Instead I am claiming that this is an indication of times to come. The biggest tech companies in Silicon Valley are not only working towards the evolution of the human mind, but they are also involved on a very deep and concrete level in global politics. In 2012 Facebook became the first Internet site with a billion users per month, and more than half a billion users visiting Facebook every day. In the US more than half of the population between 18 and 36 years old visit Facebook within a few minutes of standing up and 28% are on it before they come out of bed. Here we come to the more interesting philosophical layer of this discussion: Google and Facebook slowly became integrated parts of our brains now. New-born children already believe that even the sky is a touch screen.

AB: Yes, that seems totally right to me: it seems that Facebook is not so much about giving us what we desire but that it is actually something which changes and transforms our desires and how we articulate them and go about realizing them. So what can we do about this? It seems to me that criticisms of such things like Facebook often fall into nostalgia, simply saying that we have lost our ability to connect with people in a "real" way and that technology has spoiled things. But that isn't your position at all, so what can we do? How can we use Facebook to our advantage?

SH: The first precondition to act and change something is to recognize it. But with Facebook this is getting very difficult because we are increasingly changed by it without knowing it. I think the first question is not so much *how* to resist this but *why* should we resist it, because I think for most users of technology it is not so evident *why* we need to resist it. For instance, one user could say that Facebook helps to get connected and even revolutionaries can use Facebook to organize things, so is it so bad? To answer the question of why to resist these things we need to come back right to the beginning, to the creation of the Internet. What most people forget and what most of the biggest private companies today want to deny is that the Internet wouldn't exist without massive public funding, mostly from the US state. Why is this important? It brings us back to a very important part of Karl Marx's *Grundrisse*, which is the fragment on "the Machine" where Marx introduces the term of the "General Intellect" by saying that the problem of capitalism consists in the fact that knowledge (*epistēmē*) wouldn't be possible without the accumulation of different forms of knowledge which is the result of people unifying and getting together and creating something together – let's put it as simply as that.

The Internet is the best example of this – something that was created by a social body getting together, and slowly became privatized. To put it in more concrete terms, remember the death of Steve Jobs when newspapers all around the globe were celebrating him as the biggest "genius" of the 21st century? What people tend to forget (and you can see this in the recent biopic about "Steve Jobs") is that – I am sorry to disappoint his fans – Steve Jobs was not a genius and Mark Zuckerberg neither. What all these companies do is acquisition, acquisition, acquisition. These companies continually buy smaller companies, creating monopoly and oligopoly. It's interesting that Steve Jobs himself, in an interview back in 1983, remarked on the fact that "we speak a language that other people developed and that we use mathematics that other people evolved – that we are constantly using things that other people made." I think this is the best definition of the General Intellect: I don't think that such a thing as a "genius" exists – these things would never be possible if it was not for years and years of accumulated collective knowledge. But what capitalism is trying to tell/sell us is that Steve Jobs, Bill Gates and Mark Zuckerberg are geniuses and even humanists when in fact they are just buying more creative new companies. Perhaps their only genius was – acquisition. Did Google invent Google Maps? No. Did Google invent YouTube? No. They bought these new companies. Google would not be possible without having acquired Keyhole, which was a startup co-funded by the CIA, so again you have state support invested into Google and then you have acquisition again.

To fully answer the question of why this is a problem we could speak about Google Maps. At the beginning of 2016 Google announced that Google Maps will not only serve the search function but it will actually serve to predict the destination that its users want to go to. This really changes everything and I think it can answer to the question of why we need to resist or subvert these developments. There is a new startup called Snips, from Paris, which is working on a new AI application which will actually guess what you are going to do and provide pre-built solutions. The point is to know so much about you and what you want to do that it does it for you. I am sure that Google or Apple will acquire this company in the not-so-distant future as well. They probably already did it. In any case Google is doing this too. This is a real change because the main idea of Google was based on search but now, in a kind of paradox, you will not only have search but Google will predict the search instead of you. This changes the way we think, we desire and dream.

Let's take this example: you meet a person whom you feel attracted to on the street. Then you get basic information about the person and according to this information you can search the person and find out more about this person that you feel attracted to. If you have the name of the person you can do this: locate their Facebook profile and get a better perception of this person and according to this information you have the possibility to act and maybe to interact and ask them to have a date with you. So what does this have to do with the evolution of the human mind? Last year, Stanford published a study showing that for the first time, computers can better predict a personality than friends or family. I think this is really a sign of the future in which we already live. They did this by analyzing Facebook "likes." It starts from the assumption that the average user makes 220 likes and out of this the likes are analyzed by the computer. When the computer analyzed ten likes, it could predict the personality better than a colleague from work. When it analyzed 70 of the user's likes, the computer could predict the personality better than a friend or roommate. When it analyzed 150 likes, it could predict personality better than a family member. And finally we come back to love: when the computer analyses 300 likes (more than the average user makes) it can come very close to predicting the personality of the user as well as a spouse or lover. So it knows you better than your friends and almost as well as your spouse. The computer can use a huge amount of information and analyze it using algorithms in a few seconds. Imagine how long it would take a human to analyze 300 likes. Imagine you are trying to analyze the likes of the person you are attracted to. First, you have a lot of information to deal with and it will take you forever. Second, you have a human problem: you will probably analyze the first and second but by the time you come to the fourth like you will invest much more interpretation into this like than a computer will do. Because of this you can come to a wrong interpretation of the personality. Why is this important? It brings us to the topic of artificial intelligence.

There was another experiment recently by Google Brain in which they connected 16 thousand microprocessors, creating a neural net of a billion connections, exposed to ten million YouTube images in an attempt to see if the system could learn to identify what it saw. And you know what happened? The system figured out – on its own – what a cat is. I think this shows that we are living in the world of sci-fi and dystopian futures and that artificial intelligence is already being created. Out of machine learning from the 1960s onwards we now have the genuine creation of AI. Why should this scare us? I think finally we are coming to an answer to your question. There is a great science-fiction movie from 1970 which is called *Collossus: The Forbin Project*. It's not very famous, but the story is incredible. The story of the movie, which is set in the Cold War period, is that the US invested into an advanced supercomputer called "Colossus" which it uses to control nuclear weapons. Then this supercomputer finds out that the Russians also created a supercomputer, which is called "the Guardian." Then the next step is that the two computers establish connections and start to communicate in a binary language that the scientists cannot interpret. So the scientists cut the connection between the two computers, but then one of the computers launches a nuclear attack, forcing them to reconnect them. Eventually what happens is that the two computers, "Colossus" and "Guardian," work together to create a new supercomputer, a completely new entity, neither "Colossus" nor "Guardian." For me this film is a good prediction of things to come: it is not the Russians or the US anymore but a supercomputer which in the end runs the world. I think we are already very near this point because of the research into AI. The language that the two computers speak in this film is too fast for the scientists to understand. Here we come to Paul Virillio's thesis that speed, what he calls "dromology," is an essential political category. If you look at Wall Street today, on the one hand you have the acceleration of Wall Street where a computer can execute a trade in less than half a millionth of a second, more than a million times faster than the human mind can make a decision; on the other hand you have the increasing automation of Wall Street where algorithms are doing things that humans were doing. So a situation predicted by a science-fiction movie from the 1970s is a future that is already here. We already have computers that communicate with each other, trade with each other and interact at a speed that humans cannot understand. So eventually we will not even need humans anymore. I think what is happening, like in *Collossus: The Forbin Project*, is that we are creating something that we are not even aware that we are creating and once we realize that we have created this thing – it will already be too late.

AB: Does this have to do with technophobia and technophilia – that we are repulsed by technology and its futures but also attracted to them in very powerful ways? How do you think we should react to such technological advances that might even, without exaggerating, take over the world? What you are pointing out in the above answers is how political and corporate interests, which are increasingly one and the same thing, are very much in charge of these technological advances. So, once we recognize this, should we boycott or resist such technological advances, or should we instead try to use them in a subversive way? If so, what would that look like?

SH: That is a very interesting question and I think it is answered in Franco "Bifo" Berardi's recent book, *And: Phenomenology of the End*, which also describes these changes that are occurring. Whereas I call them evolution he calls them mutation and neo-totalitarianism. He also poses the question of whether we should resist this mutation.[19] What he says is that it is impossible to resist this mutation because any attempt to resist it would be a technophobia that is totally reactionary. So the only thing to do is enter the Network or the Machine, as it were, and try to re-program it.

Here we come back to our discussion on politics – maybe we have reached a time where *all* forms of resisting power are insufficient. Power doesn't reside in parliaments anymore. Power also doesn't entirely reside in the government anymore. Google is more powerful than any government in the world and as you will see they are even deciding who will be the next US president. But what WikiLeaks shows is that at the level of function in the Network, you can subvert it. Julian Assange, who has hacked his way into the Machine even before the Internet as we know it today existed, created WikiLeaks in 2006. Assange could easily have become another Steve Jobs or Mark Zuckerberg and could have been the CEO of a huge Silicon Valley company which would have involved the creation of a monopole, the accumulation of smaller companies and ultimately the creation of huge amounts of capital. Then, people would probably also call him a "genius." But, Assange decided to do something completely different – to create an organization that would fight these kinds of technological developments which bring us into the dystopian future. What WikiLeaks and other whistleblowers showed is that we live in surveillance capitalism where Google knows not only what we know about ourselves, but even knows what we don't know about ourselves – what we might want to know in the future, for example.

This is actually a scenario from *Minority Report* (2002), the famous sci-fi story by Philip K. Dick, then made into a movie by Stephen Spielberg. In the film Tom Cruise's character is going through the streets and a hologram appears and says something like this: "Oh, have you seen these new jeans?" and these new jeans just appear, and the hologram says: "Two weeks ago you bought these jeans so we thought that these could be your next pair." This was supposed to be science fiction, but just recently a new company has emerged called *Emotient* which is precisely dealing with this. This company measures the feelings of shoppers as they walk through the shops and experience new products. They are analyzing emotions in order to predict what the shoppers might buy, helping companies make more money by selling more products. How do they do this? They use technology involving high-definition cameras and neuro-networks which measure the subconscious emotions of the shoppers by reading the micro-expressions that unconsciously flicker across the faces of the shoppers. Does it come as a surprise that just recently, Apple acquired this company?

This brings us back to the definition of capitalism and the fact that capitalism naturally tends towards monopoly. The more Google and Apple acquire, the more powerful they become. They acquire more and more startups which actually creates the possibility of this supercomputer to create an even more powerful monopoly. In late 2015 Google bought nine drone companies after they realized that Amazon are already planning to use drones to deliver packages. These companies just become bigger and bigger, developing stronger monopolies. So to the question that you posed: how do we get out of this deadlock? I think that WikiLeaks shows a possible way to do so, by understanding these new developments and not fighting against them *per se*, but instead using technology to subvert it. On the one hand they reveal secrets as Edward Snowden did and Chelsea Manning did. Snowden showed that we live in a surveillance capitalism where you have contracts between companies like Facebook and Google and the NSA, showing that the paradigm has changed because before the government always had the big data and the hold over information, but now it is the companies that have the most information about our daily lives.

This is also why cryptography and encryption are so important. However, what you see now is that the governments are using the latest terrorist attacks in order to fight even more against cryptography and encryption. After the recent Paris attacks in 2015, for instance, the director of the FBI, James Comey suggested that encryption benefits the terrorists. The former director of the CIA James Woolsey was even more explicit: he said that after the Paris attacks Snowden has blood on his hands and should be hanged for what happened in Paris. What you can see at the moment is that the FBI and the CIA are using the terrorist actions in order to justify creating a backdoor into iPhones. In other words, we might soon be in the scenario described in the classic dystopia of Zamyatin's science-fiction novel *We*, which was published in 1921. Interestingly, it was the first novel banned by the Soviet authorities. The novel imagines a world in which everything is transparent and everyone lives in houses made out of glass. The only way to get privacy in the society is one hour per day in which you can be in private to have sex, but only on the conditions that you inform the authorities of the exact time of the rendezvous and register your sexual partner. What we have today is that we do not even have this one hour of privacy anymore because everything we do leaves a trace and the biggest Silicon Valley companies cooperate with the NSA and the state and they know everything about us. On the one hand everything is transparent, but on the other hand the actions of these companies are not transparent at all. So again, I think that organizations such as WikiLeaks are needed more than ever.

AB: So we have a difficult thing to overcome here. On the one hand we have a drive to exhibit every aspect of our identities as publicly as possible via Facebook, Twitter, Instagram and even things like Academic.edu for the universities and LinkedIn for the businesses, which ensure that no aspect of our life is not uploaded for the approval of either the Big Other or the people we can reach via the Internet. On the other hand, we at least claim to be living in an increasing fear of transparency, surveillance and panopticism which we claim that we want to avoid. So can we negotiate these drives, or why are we so driven to make things worse for ourselves?

SH: That is a good question and if we had a proper answer to that I think we could offer a solution to this problem and then we wouldn't have the problem. But let's say that narcissism is a characteristic of human beings that will surely never disappear.

We can only be aware of it, recognize it and try to change it or get rid of it. But of course what Facebook and Instagram are doing is reinforcing precisely this worst aspect of our narcissism. On Instagram people publish 80 million images per day. And – does it come as a surprise again? – Instagram has now been acquired by Facebook. They noticed that Instagram was a successful medium that was publishing 80 million images or more per day, so they simply acquired it. With Instagram, 90% of the users are under 30 years old. Most of the images published there are "selfies" which is a recent phenomenon that became huge around 2013 when the Oxford Dictionary also proclaimed "selfie" as the word of the year. Selfies are even part of politics now: there was the famous Obama selfie during the Nelson Mandela funeral and Hilary Clinton started using selfies in her campaigns. But look, with selfies there is a particular narcissism: with selfies people don't only present themselves using the selfie but they actually perceive and identify themselves through the selfie. I think this brings something new to what Christopher Lasch called "the culture of narcissism" at the end of the 1970s, which we discussed above. Then, we were far away from the time of the selfie, which has deep consequences for how we perceive ourselves and how we perceive others as well. It reinforces a narcissism that is already part of human beings and I think that future individuals and new generations to come will not even be able to act in the world without the notion of a selfie and everything that it implies. So what Facebook is actually doing is a reduction of human relationships to "likes"; it is an alienation which commodifies human beings as such.

Let's take some new economic models that seem at first glance to be unproblematic, like Airbnb and Uber. What is wrong with these? Why wouldn't someone use my apartment when I'm not there and I could earn some extra money? The problem is that every human relationship becomes a kind of transaction. With Airbnb and Uber each human relationship is commodified. This is the opposite of "sharing economy."

AB: Uber also allows you to avoid talking to the driver because all the necessary information is passed through the app, so they already know where you need to go. Also, you can check the profile of drivers, including their pictures and maybe even a bio – before you decide whether to let them drive you or not – so it really is their whole identity that is on sale, it's very much part of the product they are selling. So there is that, and also the fact that everything is automated by applications and devices probably owned by Apple and Google.

SH: Yes, it is what Grindr and Tindr are doing in emotional life. This is related to something else – the idea of "Smart Cities." This is really a process of commodifying all social relations. According to the latest projections, by 2050 more than seven billion people will live in urban areas and these large companies have realized this. We will probably have a new industrial revolution and this will be what is already being called "Smart Cities." This will involve more efficient transport, automated products, deliveries and everything via applications and devices at the touch of a button. "Smart Cities" sounds very cool, but what is really being created is the possibility of the penetration of Google and Apple into everything: the real estate, the parks, the public spaces, the total privatization of the Commons so that all social relations will be commodified. I think Uber and Airbnb point us in this direction and these biggest companies will just continue to penetrate into every aspect of our daily lives. All devices, buildings and vehicles are already embedded with electronic sensors and software and before long we will have a situation in which everything which you can imagine, everything you can see and even everything you can think of will be hyper-connected. Here we should come back to Bifo's idea of mutation.

AB: You've made some references to Berardi's idea of the "mutation" of the mind and you have a similar concept which you call the "evolution" of the mind. You also used the word "re-programming" of the mind. It seems to me that these three words have different connotations and I want to ask you about qualifying them. To me, evolution implies progression, whilst mutation implies something negative, and re-programming even implies that the mind has always been programmed technologically, which is probably my favorite of the three terms. What is happening to our minds – mutation, evolution or re-programming?

SH: This exact tension is found, once again, in the discussions of *pharmacon*. If you say "mutation" it has a negative connotation. If you say "evolution" it has not necessarily a positive connotation but a teleological one – the implication that we cannot do anything about it. Bifo is more pessimistic than me, but I agree with him that it might be already too late. If you really under-stand what Silicon Valley is about you can see that they are just rapidly buying up all the startups and assimilating them into their monopoly. We can't stop this. It is too late to stop this.

To get out of this deadlock, I think we need, first of all, to realize there is no way back. Look at the three biggest fields of investment of the biggest companies in Silicon Valley in recent years: the first is artificial intelligence (AI), the second is immor-tality and the third is virtual reality (VR). With each of these three developments, it is already too late, in the sense that all of these three are already being created, integrated and they are already changing the way that we think or even feel. They cannot be stopped now. Maybe even this book will be inadequate to discuss it – how much it will have progressed at the time when the book is published. The richest people may soon be able to upload their brains into clouds. With AI you will not even need drivers – and we can just think of the vast numbers who will lose their jobs.

Even the brokers in Wall Street will be replaced – not that I care if they lose their jobs, but they should care. I think we are already in the stage of these transformations and what Bifo or Julian Assange do is warn us, before it's too late, about where we are living. But I do use the word "evolution" because all of this seems inevitable and I think when machines will look back at human history they will see that this was all an inevitable and logical part of the evolution of the world. In order to resist all this mutation/evolution, the only solution available is to re-enter the Machine and re-program it, turn Uber and Airbnb into sharing economy, transform the privatization of the General Intellect again into something that is public, transform the concept of intellectual property in a way that would allow free exchange of knowledge, etc.

AB: Maybe to finish this we can have one final question about how we can practically move forward as individuals. So WikiLeaks is something that moves against the hegemonic politics of technology by using technology itself, but if we are not the next Julian Assange, what can we do on a more personal or individual level? Should we boycott things like Facebook or use them to subvert the situation?

SH: One of my favorite science-fiction authors, Philip K. Dick, published a novel which perfectly explains what subversion of hegemonic politics means. *Man in the High Castle*, which was recently made into a TV series, imagines a "what if…" scenario, in which the Nazis and the Japanese won the Second World War. And they have a hegemonic position by imposing their own story, the construction of this victory. Now look at the story a bit closer: what it actually shows is that hegemony always comes hand in hand with construction of a story, by giving meaning to history which then preconditions the present and what is or isn't possible in the future. This is the old question which Alice in

Wonderland posed to Humpty Dumpty: "How can words have so many meanings?" and he answered: "It depends who is the Master, and that's all." The same goes for history – its meaning depends on who is the Master. What the Resistance in Dick's novel is effectively doing is a subversion of the prevailing "status quo": by smuggling books (or movies, in the TV adaption), these courageous activists are creating a different reading and understanding of history, by which they are intervening in the present and opening a possibility of a different future. Isn't this the same as what WikiLeaks is doing? By revealing the truth, WikiLeaks is basically subverting the dominant paradigm and offering tools for resistance. It's up to us to use them.

And here we come back to the notion of subversion again. Let's agree that there is no "outside," no way to get "out" of the situation we are in. Even if you go to the most distant island, are you sure that you are not being put under surveillance, that someone on another island is not watching you on Google Earth or a drone? There is no way to get outside, wherever you go. So if we can agree on this, then we can come back to the notion of subversion and the question of what it concretely means. Take TOR for example: you don't have to use Google or Yahoo, you can use the search engine called TOR in order to go through the so-called "deep net" so that you do not leave a trace of everything you did while using the Internet. You can avoid the harvesting of information which is used not only for targeted marketing but also for surveillance and predicting behavior of all potentially subversive individuals. A possible notion of subversion is defined brilliantly by Heinz von Foerster, the godfather of cybernetics. His main rule was: "Always act in a way that increases the options." This is very similar to chess strategy. For instance, if you are trying to fight against mutation, you cannot fight it using only the existing means like Facebook, Instagram, Twitter, etc., but you need instead to take actions that increase your options. You need to use TOR and you need to use Signal or Telegram as applications on your smartphone, but at the same time you can also use Twitter. For instance, when Edward Snowden opened Twitter last year he quickly got a million users. But, on the other hand, do you know who is the most followed person on Twitter?

AB: I think it's Justin Bieber isn't it?

SH: You are very close! He is second. The first is Katy Perry and the third is Taylor Swift. So if you just look at those three you get a good picture of today's situation. Obama is fourth, and then you have Rihanna, Britney Spears and so on. So what does this show? It shows that if Katy Perry, who has more than 80 million followers, was to endorse Hilary Clinton tomorrow then this would have a significant influence. It is a power that can really decide elections. On the other hand, WikiLeaks has over three million followers itself and Edward Snowden has over two million more, so it shows that this power can also be used for subversion by those who oppose the "mutation" that is going on. However, I think this still isn't enough. We should change also our daily lives. Next time we use Apple or open a profile or install a new application, we should think about it before we click "I agree." I think 90% of people do not even read "conditions" they agree to and they simply click without thinking. When you log into a Wi-Fi in a hotel or an airport you agree to cookies, surveillance and monitoring, and you do it willingly, often without even knowing it or not really caring. So I think people can still do a lot by trying to be much more aware and make small steps in the right direction. You can use encryption, you can use TOR, you can use Signal or Telegram, for instance, so that your communication is much safer, and you can make sure that you don't opt in to surveillance when you have been given the choice. This is a way to resist the "mutation." This is, of course, just one small step, but at least it is a step in the right direction.

Last but not least, concluding what subversion could mean,

we should say that in order to subvert something, you need to understand it. In order to subvert the Machine or the Network, you need to get inside of it. If we are not able to understand what is happening today we are not going to be able to subvert or change anything about it. So the only way to change anything – and this is the reason why philosophy is more important than ever: because it gives us the possibility of understanding – is to understand the world around us, the future which is already here. And by understanding we can, maybe, change it.

At the same time, even if it sounds paradoxical, when you are in the middle of a process of change you are also able to understand better. And this is why I believe philosophy and praxis must go together. By the very act of walking we are creating new paths.

Interviewer's Reflections

At the end of my interview series with Srećko, the thing that struck me most powerfully was that what had set out as three separate conversations had become something that could be much more useful as one continuous discussion. This pointed to one of the most forceful parts of Srećko's project, which has been to show how interrelated and connected apparently separate categories can be. His work points out that the illusion of separation between categories (love and politics, politics and technology, technology and love) can be a dangerous ideological tactic which prevents us from understanding our historical moment and doing anything about it.

In *The Radicality of Love*, for example, he shows that even the most intimate human emotions and impulses, the things that seem most powerfully our own, the things that feel most "free," have become *technologized*, so that our very private consciousness (as well as our public one) has evolved and transformed in the technological age. At the same time there is always a politics to this technology and to the transformations it enacts in us, a corporate and political hegemony structuring the subjects that we are becoming. Keeping these interrelations quiet can serve the hegemonic trends in our discourse. To recognize these connections between politics, technology and love and to understand them, I learned through these interviews, is already to begin the difficult task of subversion. I hope this book will, at the very least, start a radical conversation about the intersections between our three "topics."

Many suggestions and possible solutions to the political problems of today emerged in the first conversation on "politics," but there were also, inevitably, many unanswered questions. One sticking point, for example, was on the question of how to deal with a psychoanalytic disavowal found in the Left today, who know very well that nationalism is bad but continue to celebrate events and discourses that involve identification with national identity. In that first interview this problem remained an open one which we did not directly answer, but towards the conclusion of the second interview on the subject of "love," something of a possible solution emerged involving a revolution in the relationship with the other (in this case the other of another nation) which would allow us to accept otherness rather than continue to seek sameness and narcissistic reflective identification in the other. As Srećko's discussion of Che Guevara shows us, solutions can be found by treating politics and love not as separate spheres but as inseparable structures.

Looking forward, the need for further work on technology seems to be the most important consideration, as indeed it is the current focus of Srećko's work, which currently involves close collaboration with Julian Assange. As I write this I look forward to an upcoming conversation between Srećko, Assange and Varoufakis and cannot resist the implication that Srecko = love, Varoufakis = politics and Assange = technology. That these three are talking is already an important move, and in my opinion we can thank Srećko for this combination. His written work has thematically forced these categories together and his organization on the ground has consistently worked to bring voices together who need to collaborate and whose collaboration can move things forward for the Left today.

At several times in the interviews Srećko refers to the recent work of the philosopher Franco "Bifo" Berardi, whose arguments can be found most directly in his book *And: Phenomenology of the End*, which deserves another mention here. Berardi's argument is that technology has mutated consciousness and that – whilst it may already be too late to do anything about this, should we even desire to do so – it is imperative that we understand these processes that are happening/have happened to consciousness itself. Whilst Srećko refers to an "evolution" in consciousness – a difference I asked him about in the third section – he and Berardi are working together here as part of a project to encourage a different kind of awareness about cognition and the changes that occur in thinking itself. There is not a lot of attention paid to these processes inside or outside of philosophy, and one thing I hope readers will take away from our interview is a strong sense of the importance of these mutations and a renewed desire to study what it means to think in our particular moment, something I have resolved to study further myself as a direct result of these interviews.

Where I would like to close the book is with reference to the continuing problems facing the Left today, something that we are tasked with overcoming. Whilst the reader can probably object that there is no single clear agenda to be found in these pages that describes precisely how to work against the dominant hegemonic and corporate trends with which we must compete, I would like to suggest that this is the beginning of a battle which will not necessarily be long but will certainly be huge. The first step, as Srećko argues here, must be to understand. Srećko finished the interview with a reference to Marx's famous statement at the very end of the "Theses on Feuerbach": "The philosophers have only interpreted the world, in various ways; the point is to change it."

Usually taken as something like a critique of philosophy, or a claim that philosophy is never enough, the point here was to reclaim Marx's phrase as a reminder that understanding must precede action and that philosophy, often dismissed as the thought of the past, has never been more necessary than it is today. Unlike many philosophers, Srećko is not open to the criticism that he is all thought and no action. Srećko's own career could not be described as philosophy without action, and as came out in the interviews, he has been involved in demonstrations, occupations and practical political movements across the world pretty continuously for the last decade. His work is always at the forefront of the technological and political, as his recent work with Yanis Varoufaskis and Julian Assange shows. But throughout all this much-needed political action, collective organization and technological subversion is the continuing need for philosophy, the continuing need to think and to understand, before, during and after our actions.

Srećko struck me as someone whose work is really doing something in today's unarable political climate, more so than I could have imagined before these interviews. It also struck me as a force that is unusually optimistic in comparison to most of the discussions found in our political climate today. The Left today is certainly in a kind of crisis, and I am writing this reflection in the direct aftermath of the 2016 New Left Forum in New York, when Slavoj Žižek was heckled by other apparent Leftists, plunging the debate into a kind of in-fighting and precluding collaborative work and solidarity against our real enemies. Srećko's work, like Berardi's, follows the belief that we are in an unprecedented crisis today, even what Agamben calls *stasis* or what we could call a Third World War, the idea with which these interviews began. Yet, this crisis, which we are in the midst of, means not that hope is lost but that contributions are needed more than ever; that in a global situation of crisis and war, there is something to fight over: a chance for the Left to do something. If we see Srećko's point that we are in a situation where the "old" has passed and the "new" has not yet fully emerged, I can imagine no more powerful call-to-arms for the Left today. To take up this battle is to combat political, technological and corporate hegemony in all areas, even those most intimate and personal to us.

In his New Left Forum discussion this year, Slavoj Žižek comments on the tight control of media – both technological and traditional – and sees in the seemingly desperate situation scope and hope for radical effort: "There is still hope because the more tightly things are controlled, the more those in control get into a panic and the more easily they are wounded. [...] The more our enemy controls the public space, the more it is vulnerable." This statement rings true when it comes to much of Srećko's work and much of the subversive work that he discusses in the interviews – take WikiLeaks as one example (one Žižek also comments on in the lecture quoted above). Such powerful tools are opened up to us by technology and by a political and corporate hegemony over that technology. With that situation in place and because of it, we can use technology for genuinely subversive causes; we can, to quote Srećko from above, be aware of all these technological developments, and re-enter the machine in order to re-program it.

This is not an easy task, and it will take immense personal sacrifice from many people. This was another of the things that struck me most forcefully in my interviews with Srećko, as I intimated in the introduction. In the six weeks over which we recorded the initial tapes it became apparent to me that Srećko had no fixed abode, and interviews were recorded in Germany, Croatia and London, while we were also in touch while he was in Greece, France and Morocco, among other places. It's really impossible for me to overstate just how hectic and busy Srećko's life is. Each of our meetings, of course, was facilitated by the latest technology which connected us from wherever we were. We used it, at least, to create this text. Perhaps that is part of a politics of subversion. The work of collaborating, disseminating and developing a left-wing platform is obviously not an easy one and, whilst we might not all make the personal sacrifices that Srećko has made, it will need a lot more work from all of us, both on the ground and in the cloud.

Yet, Srećko does not see any of this as any kind of sacrifice. He admitted to me that in the last two months while working on this book he has "traveled like a madman" through more than 20 countries. At one point he even commented that he was visiting "only six countries in the next ten days" and that therefore he would have some time for our book, as if that signified a let-up in his hectic schedule. Srećko was clear that he does not – even if he does not have a permanent address, see his parents or sister as much as he would want, nor have the chance to do "normal" stuff "normal" people do – see this as sacrifice. Instead, he sees it as a gift. He told me that in the last couple of weeks he had many new friends – from PJ Harvey to Patti Smith, and many many unknown refugees and activists from Calais to Idomeni – and this is the biggest gift he has. Using the title of a PJ Harvey song, Srećko says that he believes by all this, including our little book, we are building a "Community of Hope."

Srećko's work, to my mind, is both a successful attempt to begin this work, and a powerful call-to-arms for the rest of us to join it, encouraging us to develop a new pan-European and global community on the Left and, with it, a new future.

– Alfie Bown

Endnotes

1   https://www.opendemocracy.net/sre%C4%87ko-horvat
    /europe-are-there-nazis-living-on-moon

2   See, for example, https://www.theguardian.com/comment-
    isfree/2014/jun/16/pope-world-cup-balkans-croatian-players
    -francis

3   http://www.jergovic.com/sumnjivo-lice/cinizam-gorana-rad
    mana-protivan-je-zdravom-drustvu/

4   Slavoj Žižek and Srećko Horvat, *What Does Europe Want?: The
    Union and its Discontents* (London: Istros Books, 2013), p. 60.

5   See Antonio Gramsci, *Selections from Prison Notebooks: State
    and Civil Society* (London: Lawrence & Wishart, 1971), p. 556.

6   See Giorgio Agamben, *Stasis: Civil War as a Political Paradigm*,
    trans. Nicholas Heron (California: Stanford University Press,
    2015).

7   See Mark Fisher, *Capitalist Realism: Is There No Alternative?*
    (Winchester and Washington: Zero Books, 2009), pp. 1–3.

8   Walter Benjamin, "Leftwing Melancholy" in *Walter Benjamin:
    Selected Writings: 1927–1934*, ed. Michael W. Jennings,
    Howard Eiland and Gary Smith (Cambridge, MA: Harvard
    University Press, 1996), pp. 423–7.

9   http://eutopiamagazine.eu/en/sre%C4%87ko-horvat/
    speakers-corner/refugees-ikea-shelters-and-why-solidarity-
    not-proper-answer#sthash.kGzH3DpF.dpuf

10 http://analyzegreece.gr/news/item/103-srecko-horvat-
    greece-and-the-temptation-of-syriza

11 The full text of this can be found at https://yanisvaroufak
    is.eu/2013/12/10/confessions-of-an-erratic-marxist-in-the-
    midst-of-a-repugnant-european-crisis/#_edn1

12 See Srećko Horvat, *The Radicality of Love* (London: Polity,
    2015).

13 Christopher Lasch, *The Culture of Narcissism* (London: W. W.

Norton, 1979) p. 61.

14   See Alain Badiou, *In Praise of Love* (London: Serpent's Tail, 2012).

15   See Carl Schmitt, *The Concept of the Political*, trans. George Schwab (Chicago: University of Chicago Press, 2007).

16   Here Horvat refers to Slavoj Žižek's 2008 discussion of "unknown knowns" which is available at http://www.the guardian.com/commentisfree/2008/jun/28/wildlife.conservation

17   This was Heidegger's first public speaking event since the end of the war. These four lectures were published later under the now well-known title of "The Question Concerning Technology."

18   Freidrich Hölderlin, *Sämtliche Werke*, vol IV, quoted in Martin Heidegger, *Off the Beaten Track*, (Cambridge: Cambridge University Press, 2002) p. 222 (p. 190).

19   See Franco "Bifo" Berardi, *And: Phenomenology of the End – Sensibility and Connective Mutation* (South Pasadena, CA: Semiotext(e), 2015).

Zero Books
CULTURE, SOCIETY & POLITICS

Contemporary culture has eliminated the concept and public figure of the intellectual. A cretinous anti-intellectualism presides, cheer-led by hacks in the pay of multinational corporations who reassure their bored readers that there is no need to rouse themselves from their stupor. Zer0 Books knows that another kind of discourse - intellectual without being academic, popular without being populist - is not only possible: it is already flourishing. Zer0 is convinced that in the unthinking, blandly consensual culture in which we live, critical and engaged theoretical reflection is more important than ever before.

If you have enjoyed this book, why not tell other readers by posting a review on your preferred book site. Recent bestsellers from Zer0 Books are:

In the Dust of This Planet
Horror of Philosophy vol. 1
Eugene Thacker
In the first of a series of three books on the Horror of Philosophy, In the Dust of This Planet offers the genre of horror as a way of thinking about the unthinkable.
Paperback: 978-1-84694-676-9 ebook: 978-1-78099-010-1

Capitalist Realism
Is there no alternative?
Mark Fisher
An analysis of the ways in which capitalism has presented itself as the only realistic political-economic system.
Paperback: 978-1-84694-317-1 ebook: 978-1-78099-734-6

Rebel Rebel
Chris O'Leary
David Bowie: every single song. Everything you want to know, everything you didn't know.
Paperback: 978-1-78099-244-0 ebook: 978-1-78099-713-1

Cartographies of the Absolute
Alberto Toscano, Jeff Kinkle
An aesthetics of the economy for the twenty-first century.
Paperback: 978-1-78099-275-4 ebook: 978-1-78279-973-3

Malign Velocities
Accelerationism and Capitalism
Benjamin Noys
Long listed for the Bread and Roses Prize 2015, Malign Velocities argues against the need for speed, tracking acceleration as the symptom of the on-going crises of capitalism.
Paperback: 978-1-78279-300-7 ebook: 978-1-78279-299-4

Meat Market
Female flesh under Capitalism
Laurie Penny
A feminist dissection of women's bodies as the fleshy fulcrum of capitalist cannibalism, whereby women are both consumers and consumed.
Paperback: 978-1-84694-521-2 ebook: 978-1-84694-782-7

Poor but Sexy
Culture Clashes in Europe East and West
Agata Pyzik
How the East stayed East and the West stayed West.
Paperback: 978-1-78099-394-2 ebook: 978-1-78099-395-9

Romeo and Juliet in Palestine
Teaching Under Occupation
Tom Sperlinger
Life in the West Bank, the nature of pedagogy and the role of a
university under occupation.
Paperback: 978-1-78279-637-4 ebook: 978-1-78279-636-7

Sweetening the Pill
or How we Got Hooked on Hormonal Birth Control
Holly Grigg-Spall
Has contraception liberated or oppressed women? Sweetening
the Pill breaks the silence on the dark side of hormonal contraception.
Paperback: 978-1-78099-607-3 ebook: 978-1-78099-608-0

Why Are We The Good Guys?
Reclaiming your Mind from the Delusions of Propaganda
David Cromwell
A provocative challenge to the standard ideology that Western
power is a benevolent force in the world.
Paperback: 978-1-78099-365-2 ebook: 978-1-78099-366-9

Readers of ebooks can buy or view any of these bestsellers by
clicking on the live link in the title. Most titles are published
in paperback and as an ebook. Paperbacks are available in
traditional bookshops. Both print and ebook formats are
available online.

Find more titles and sign up to our readers' newsletter at
http://www.johnhuntpublishing.com/culture-and-politics

Follow us on Facebook at
https://www.facebook.com/ZeroBooks
and Twitter at https://twitter.com/Zer0Books